Contents

List of figures and tables

Figures

Essential Data Skills – Leisure and Tourism

London: TSO

Published by TSO (The Stationery Office) and available from:

Online
www.tso.co.uk/bookshop

Mail, Telephone, Fax & E-mail
TSO
PO Box 29, Norwich NR3 1GN
Telephone orders/General enquiries: 0870 6005522
Fax orders: 0870 6005533
E-mail: book.orders@tso.co.uk
Textphone: 0870 240 3701

TSO Shops
123 Kingsway, London WC2B 6PQ
020 7242 6393 Fax 020 7242 6394
68–69 Bull Street, Birmingham B4 6AD
0121 236 9696 Fax 0121 236 9699
9–21 Princess Street, Manchester M60 8AS
0161 834 7201 Fax 0161 833 0634
16 Arthur Street, Belfast BT1 4GD
028 9023 8451 Fax 028 9023 5401
18–19, High Street, Cardiff CF10 1PT
029 2039 5548 Fax 029 2038 4347
71 Lothian Road, Edinburgh EH3 9AZ
0870 606 5566 Fax 0870 606 5588

TSO Accredited Agents
(see Yellow Pages)

and through good booksellers

The information contained in this publication is believed to be correct at the time of manufacture. Whilst care has been taken to ensure that the information is accurate, the publisher can accept no responsibility for any errors or omissions or for changes to the details given.

Paul Downward and Les Lumsdon have asserted their moral rights under the Copyright, Designs and Patents Act 1988, to be identified as the authors of this work.

Produced in collaboration with the Office for National Statistics, Room B1/09, 1 Drummond Gate, London SW1V 2QQ

A CIP catalogue record for this book is available from the British Library
A Library of Congress CIP catalogue record has been applied for

First published 2005

ISBN 0 11 703572 6

Printed in the United Kingdom by The Stationery Office, London
ID151701 09/05 315631 19585

Tables

Acknowledgements

The editors would like to acknowledge the efforts made by contributors to this volume. The opportunity costs involved in contributing to edited books is large. This is both in terms of the time constraints facing those working in various sports, leisure and tourism agencies, and because academics face real resource costs in not concentrating entirely on writing academic papers because of the Research Assessment Exercise.

The editors would also like to thank Alistair Dawson for checking and proof reading the entire manuscript in various versions, and for Pat Broad at the ONS, and Julie Pointer and Janine Eves at TSO for expediting the production of the volume.

1 Introduction

Dr Paul Downward Institute of Sport and Leisure Policy, Loughborough University
Professor Les Lumsdon Lancashire Business School, University of Central Lancashire

Statistical data are a valuable resource for those taking decisions in the sports, leisure and tourism industries and National Statistics provides key data in this sector. This book:

- illustrates how National Statistics can be employed to analyse various aspects of the sports, leisure and tourism industries
- provides information on finding useful statistics from inexpensive official sources
- gives guidance in finding the most appropriate data for different purposes
- explains commonly used statistical definitions and conventions of measurement in the presentation of National Statistics
- illustrates how data can be analysed appropriately and effectively in order to provide an understanding of the sport, leisure and tourism markets, and thereby inform decision-making in this area.

Written by an experienced team of professionals, consultants and academics, who are well versed in the analysis of the sport, leisure and tourism sectors of the economy, this book is aimed at helping those who need to use statistical data as part of their daily work. It will be relevant to those working in market research, demand forecasting and strategy, and to those making operational management decisions or engaged in project work generally. It assumes no prior knowledge of statistical methods.

The book is divided into three parts. Part 1 covers the availability of statistics relevant for the analysis of sports, leisure and tourism sectors. In Chapter 2, Paul Allin provides an overview of National Statistics. Beginning with an introduction to the organisation and collection of National Statistics, Allin covers the main sources and points of contact for potential users of data. He discusses key issues associated with measuring components of economic activity,

particularly in an international context, and provides an overview of the National Statistics that are available to help determine the economic and social contribution of leisure and tourism. There are not many National Statistics products dedicated to this sector, although various sets of statistics can be drawn together from National Statistics products and databases in order to build a picture of leisure and tourism. A key feature of the remainder of the book is to give examples of how this can be done.

In Chapter 3, Dr Brian Hay provides a discussion of complementary information on tourism statistics. This is key background information because statistics on tourism published by the national tourist boards are not, at the time of writing, part of National Statistics. It is clear, however, that these growing sectors of the economy will become more important in the future. The range of surveys and details of their aims, methodology and data availability are described and working definitions of concepts provided.

Parts 2 and 3 cover the 'twin blades' of demand and supply in the sports, leisure and tourism markets. Part 2 begins with a discussion about how demand for these activities can be explained. In Chapter 4, Dr Paul Downward uses official data to analyse the consumer's decision to participate in sports, leisure and tourism activities and produces a general framework within which one can understand the demand for them. He outlines how various theories of demand may be related and suggests a common structure of models. It examines conceptual and measurement issues associated with modelling participation. Then the chapter shows how descriptive and inferential insights about participation can easily be established from official data, but important caveats are attached to the use of commercially produced data. In Chapter 5 Dr Ramesh Durbarry and Professor Thea Sinclair show

how data can be used to describe and quantify the demand for tourism, using the UK as an example. Their chapter explains in detail how models can be used to estimate the extent to which demand changes in response to changes in key economic variables.

In Chapter 6 the emphasis changes from explaining demand towards forecasting demand. Alistair Dawson briefly reviews the complexity of markets in tourism and considers how this affects forecasting. In particular he considers how tourist activity is currently measured and possible alternative ways of doing this. Dawson discusses simple methods of time-series forecasting and applies them to official data. Dawson shows how it is very difficult to predict economic events accurately and to make effective use of such predictions.

This theme is continued in Chapter 7, where Professor Chris Gratton and Themis Kokolakakis of the Leisure Industries Research Centre, based at Sheffield Hallam University, illustrate the use of secondary data for the analysis and forecasting of consumer expenditure on leisure. The authors prepare such forecasts for annual publication in 'Leisure Forecasts'. The chapter outlines the basic approach used to produce forecasts and analyses the main factors affecting consumer expenditure on leisure and how they changed over the last 25 years of the last century. The chapter discusses how the leisure market and its various subsectors are defined and gives an overview of the output of the forecasting models produced in early 2002 for the forecast period 2002–6. The chapter then concludes by reviewing the lessons learned in trying to forecast leisure expenditure.

In Part 3, the focus of analysis shifts to the supply side of the sports, leisure and tourism markets. In Chapter 8, Dr Brian Davies argues that the supply environment is less well served by official data than the demand side of the market. He presents a theoretical framework that can be used to produce an understanding of market structure using official data; he then examines in detail how one can measure the business environment empirically, in particular industrial concentration, to generate an understanding of the structure of competition in relevant markets.

Complementing this structural emphasis, in Chapter 9 Professor Les Lumsdon and Professor R Elwyn Owen consider how official data can be used to understand segmentation in markets. They discuss the related issues of why companies and organisations segment markets in sports, leisure and tourism, how these segments can be measured and the limitations of segmentation. Finally they discuss how the concepts of segmentation, targeting and positioning are related. The ideas are applied to a case study of tourism in Wales.

In summary, without being exhaustive, it is hoped that this book illustrates critically how official data can play an active role in understanding markets in sports, leisure and tourism. The authors show that there are no dedicated sources dealing with statistics relating to sports, leisure or tourism, and that more comprehensive data are available on the demand side of markets than on the supply side. Yet there is already much that official statistics can offer the decision-maker and further data will be available in the future.

Part I

The availability of statistics relevant for the analysis of the sports, leisure and tourism sectors

2 Understanding National Statistics

Paul Allin Director of the Integration and Harmonisation Division, Office for National Statistics

Focus questions

- What are National Statistics?
- Where does leisure and tourism fit within National Statistics?
- How can you access National Statistics?
- Could satellite accounts aid the analysis of tourism?
- How is economic activity measured and valued?

Introduction

Statistics relevant to leisure and tourism are available from a wide variety of sources. This chapter concentrates on those official statistics that are designated National Statistics. The aim of having a set of National Statistics is to provide an accurate, up-to-date, comprehensive and meaningful picture of the economy and society and to support all users, whether in government, business, research, education, the media or elsewhere. The essential task is to deliver statistics that command the trust and confidence of the public. Quality is assessed in various ways, for example the fact that National Statistics are freely available to everyone. Among the very large set of National Statistics are key economic and social indicators, such as the gross domestic product (GDP) of the country and estimates of the size and distribution of the domestic population. The set of National Statistics therefore provides a comprehensive description of the economic, social and environmental context within which leisure and tourism activities take place.

This chapter provides an overview of National Statistics. Beginning with an introduction to the organisation and collection of National Statistics, the chapter then covers the main points of contact for users. Key issues associated with measuring components of economic activity, particularly in an international context, are then discussed. The chapter finishes with an overview of the National Statistics that are available to help determine the economic and social contribution of leisure and tourism. The chapter prepares the ground for the detailed studies of different aspects of leisure and tourism that follow.

National Statistics

The UK has a highly developed set of 'official statistics', that is, statistics that are produced and published by government departments. It is a decentralised system, in which the Office for National Statistics (ONS) plays a major role. ONS is an 'executive agency' within government and it is accountable to Parliament through the Chancellor of the Exchequer. ONS publishes key economic and social statistics, including compendium publications such as the annual volume *Social Trends*. In addition, all government departments and the devolved administrations publish official statistics relevant to their areas of responsibility. For example, HM Customs and Excise publishes detailed statistics on the value and volume of international trade in goods, because they are the department responsible for collecting the relevant duty and tax.

National Statistics form a subset of all official statistics, effectively a brand that was launched in June 2000. A white paper in 1999, 'Building Trust in Statistics', set out the government's intention to improve the quality of official statistics and, equally important, the perception of the quality of official statistics.

The primary aim of having a set of National Statistics is to provide an accurate, up-to-date, comprehensive and meaningful picture of the economy and society and to support the formulation and monitoring of economic and social policies by government at all levels. The producers of National Statistics also aim to provide business with a statistical service that promotes efficient functioning of commerce and industry, and to provide researchers, analysts and other customers with a statistical service that assists their work and studies. Box 2.1 shows the main avenues for users to obtain National Statistics or information about them.

Box 2.2 explains how to obtain computer readable data. Some data obtained in this way are made use of in subsequent chapters.

Box 2.1

How to obtain National Statistics

The main way of obtaining National Statistics publications, data or any information about National Statistics is via the National Statistics website www.statistics.gov.uk.

You can also contact the National Statistics Customer Contact Centre:

Email: info@statistics.gov.uk
Tel: 0845 601 3034

The devolution of powers within the United Kingdom has added a degree of complexity to the statistical picture. The UK remains a single member state within the European Union, for example, and many statistics are routinely compiled for the UK as a whole. Other statistics are compiled within the different countries of the UK. For example, three separate censuses of population and housing were conducted – in Scotland, Northern Ireland, and England and Wales – in April 2001. There is close liaison between the various producers of National Statistics so that consistent, UK-wide statistics can be produced where appropriate. In the case of the censuses, these were held on the same date and conducted in the same way. The census forms were largely composed of a common set of questions, with differences in the part of the form dealing with national identity, ethnicity and religion.

Box 2.2

National Statistics data in computer-readable form

National Statistics Online, the website shown in Box 2.1, is the official UK government source for statistical data and metadata, from national to local level. It provides a wealth of regularly updated statistical material and is free of charge. The content and design of National Statistics Online reflect user research and analysis of usage.

Among the site's features are:

- integrated search facility, available from every page
- index of contents, allowing you to find stories or articles, data or metadata by topic
- searchable database of articles from ONS journals such as *Economic Trends*
- a layer of plain-language statistical stories, telling you what you need to know about the state of Britain.

The press release and Time Series Data areas, already many people's primary source of new statistical data, have been enhanced but function exactly as before. The name 'StatBase' may be gone, but its vast collection of information from across government is only a click away, wherever you are on the new site.

For more details of these services please contact:
Online Services Branch
Office for National Statistics
B1/12, 1 Drummond Gate
London SW1V 2QQ
Tel: 020 7533 5677
Email: statbase@statistics.gov.uk

A number of National Statistics are produced in order to comply with European Union regulations or directives, or to honour commitments to other international organisations, such as the Organisation for Economic Co-operation and Development (OECD). Statistics can only be compared between different countries, or aggregated to produce European totals, if they are compiled according to consistent definitions and on similar bases. These specifications are invariably agreed as part of the process to establish the European legislation requiring the statistics to be compiled. Other international standards apply. For example, there is a standard industrial classification that allows for businesses to be categorised in a consistent and meaningful way; this is discussed in Chapter 8.

The main components of National Statistics

The main components of the infrastructure to produce National Statistics are:

- a framework document
- the responsibilities of ministers in departments and in the devolved administrations
- an independent statistics commission
- the national statistician
- statistical heads of profession in departments and administrations
- a code of practice and quality standards.

The framework document was published in June 2000. It sets out the aims and objectives for National Statistics, and describes in some detail the roles and responsibilities of key players who direct and guide the work leading to the production of National Statistics. These key players together are charged with:

- improving quality and relevance of National Statistics
- improving public confidence in National Statistics
- operating the production of National Statistics efficiently
- co-ordinating across governments, including the devolved administrations.

Ministers are accountable for determining the scope of National Statistics and for determining statistical work programmes and resources. The Chancellor of the Exchequer is the Minister for National Statistics and is responsible for appointing the chairman and members of the Statistics Commission, and the National Statistician. In practice, the Chancellor delegates day-to-day responsibility for National Statistics to the Economic Secretary to the Treasury, as the Minister responsible for the ONS.

The Statistics Commission is an independent body in that it is separate from ministers and the producers of National Statistics. The Commission is a non-executive advisory body. Its main responsibilities include representing the views of users and data suppliers in commenting on the National Statistics work programme and commenting on the quality of National Statistics. The Commission operates in a transparent and open way, which in practice means that all correspondence to and from the Commission is published on its website (www.statscom.org.uk).

The National Statistician is the Head of National Statistics, the Head of the Government Statistical Service (which is the professional grouping of all official statisticians across departments and administrations), Director of the ONS and the UK Government's chief professional advisor on statistical matters. The National Statistician has professional responsibility for the quality of the outputs comprising National Statistics and maintains and publishes the National Statistics Code of Practice to assist in this. The code of practice was launched in October 2002 and is available on the National Statistics website (www.statistics.gov.uk). The code is supported by more detailed protocols that specify how key principles addressed in the code are put into practice. In future, protocols will cover aspects of National Statistics such as release practices, quality management, data sharing and confidentiality, respondent burden and revisions. There is a designated head of profession in each department or administration producing National Statistics, who is responsible for professional integrity.

The set of National Statistics is organised into 12 themes:

- agriculture, fishing and forestry
- commerce, energy and industry
- crime and justice
- the economy
- education and training
- health and care
- labour market
- natural and built environment
- population and migration
- social and welfare
- transport, travel and tourism
- 'other' National Statistics.

Tourism is mentioned explicitly and leisure is covered by the social and welfare theme.

The first work programme for National Statistics was published in 2001. This describes the main outputs within each theme and sets out the developments proposed over the next five years. The work programme also lists the quality reviews of National Statistics outputs. Quality reviews are a rolling programme of work to review, and improve if necessary, all National Statistics outputs and to identify unmet statistical needs.

The economy and the National Accounts

Each year the Office for National Statistics compiles and publishes the Blue Book, which presents the full system of the UK National Accounts. The National Accounts are the economic accounts for the United Kingdom and show the relationships between resources, production and consumption. The National Accounts formally record and describe economic activity in the UK and are used to support the formulation and monitoring of economic and social policies. The accounts are compiled according to internationally agreed conventions. The accounts are based on the European System of Accounts 1995 (ESA95), itself based on the United Nations System of National Accounts 1993 (SNA93), which is being adopted by national statistical offices throughout the world. Information on the National Accounts can be accessed at www.statistics.gov.uk/nationalaccounts.

Gross domestic product (GDP) is arguably the most important aggregate or summary statistic for purposes of economic analysis and comparison over time within the National Accounts. It is defined as the value of the sum of all economic activity that takes place on UK territory. We need to set some basic definitions, namely:

- the limits of the UK national economy – defined in terms of economic territory, residency and centre of economic interest
- economic activity – the production to be included is said to be within a 'production boundary'
- what price is used to value the products of economic activity

- estimation or imputation of values for non-monetary transactions
- the rest of the world – differentiating between national, domestic and overseas activity.

Full descriptions of the National Accounting rules and concepts are provided in *United Kingdom National Accounts – The Blue Book* and in the reference manual *Concepts, Sources and Methods*. Consult those reference works for detailed explanations; a summary overview is given below.

The limits of the national economy: economic territory, residence and centre of economic interest

The economy of the United Kingdom is made up of institutional units that have a centre of economic interest in the UK economic territory. These units are known as resident units and it is their transactions that are recorded in the UK National Accounts. The UK economic territory comprises:

- Great Britain and Northern Ireland (the geographic territory administered by the UK Government, within which persons, goods, services and capital move freely)
- any free zones, including bonded warehouses and factories under UK Customs control
- the national air space, UK territorial waters and the UK sector of the continental shelf.

It excludes the offshore islands – the Channel Islands and the Isle of Man – which are not members of the European Union and are therefore not subject to the same fiscal and monetary authorities as the rest of the United Kingdom.

Within ESA95, the definition of economic territory also includes territorial conclaves in the rest of the world (such as embassies, military bases, scientific stations and so on used by the British Government with the formal political agreement of the governments in which these units are located). Economic territory excludes any extraterritorial conclaves (parts of the UK geographic territory like embassies and US military bases used by the government agencies of other countries).

Centre of economic interest and residency

An institutional unit has a centre of economic interest and is a resident of the UK when, from a location within the UK economic territory, it engages and intends to continue engaging in economic activities on a significant scale. By location, we include dwellings, places of production or premises. Economic activity can be intended to continue indefinitely or for a finite period: one year or more is used as a guideline.

Travellers, cross-border and seasonal workers, crews of ships and aircraft and students studying overseas are residents of their home countries and remain members of their households. However, an individual who leaves the UK for a year or more (excepting outpatients receiving medical treatment) ceases to be a member of a UK resident household and becomes a non-resident, even on home visits.

Economic activity: what production is included?

It is important to be clear about what is defined as economic activity. In its widest sense it could cover all activities resulting in the production of goods or services and so encompass some activities that are very difficult to measure. For example, estimates of smuggling of alcoholic drink and tobacco products, and the output, expenditure and income directly generated by that activity, are now included in the Blue Book.

In practice a 'production boundary' is defined, inside which are all the economic activities taken to contribute to economic performance. These activities range from agriculture and manufacturing, through service-producing activities (for example financial services, or hotels and catering), to the provision of health, education, public administration and defence.

Housework is an example of activity outside the production boundary, and thus excluded from the National Accounts. Work such as cooking meals, washing the car or looking after children, carried out by household members, is not counted, even though other households pay for these services to be undertaken by non-household members (which is

counted in the National Accounts). Chapter 4 refers to the importance of these distinctions in understanding the demand for sports, leisure and tourism. Housework and other similar activities are included in the Household Satellite Accounts launched by ONS in April 2002. 'Satellite' indicates an extension to the conventional national accounts. Such supplementary accounts were recognised in the latest version of the United Nations standard system for national accounts.

What price is used to value the products of economic activity?

In the UK, there are a number of different prices used to value inputs and outputs shown in tables in the National Accounts. This depends on the treatment of taxes and subsidies on products and trade and transport margins. These prices are:

- basic prices – the cost of production after any subsidies (this is the preferred method of valuing output because basic prices reflect the amount received by the producer for a unit of good or services, minus any taxes payable, plus any subsidy receivable on that unit as a consequence of production or sale; thus the only taxes included in the price will be taxes on the output process, such as business rates or vehicle excise duty, which are not specifically levied on the production of a unit of output)
- producers' prices – equal basic prices, plus those taxes paid (other than VAT or similar deductible taxes invoiced for the output sold) per unit of output, less any subsidies received per unit of output
- purchasers' (or market) prices – essentially these are the prices paid by the purchaser and include transport costs, trade margins and taxes (unless the taxes are deductible by the purchaser).

What are current and constant prices?

Some of the tables in the Blue Book are in 'current' prices and some are in 'constant' prices. When looking at the change in the economy over time the main concern is usually whether more goods and services are actually being produced now than at some time in the past. If we do not make any adjustments, then when we measure GDP in a particular year we are measuring it at the prices current to that year. Over time, changes in current price GDP show changes in the monetary value of the components of GDP. These changes in value can reflect changes in both price and volume. It is therefore difficult to establish how much of an increase in the series is due either to increased activity in the economy or to an increase in the price level. As a result, when looking at the real growth in the economy over time, it is usual to look at the volume, or constant price, estimates of gross domestic products.

In constant price series, transactions are revalued to a constant price level using the average prices of the selected year, known as the base year. In most cases, the revaluation, also known as deflation, is carried out by using price indices such as component series of the Retail Prices Index or Producer Price Index to deflate current price series at a detailed level of disaggregation. The importance of making these adjustments is highlighted in Chapter 5.

Sectors and industries

The National Accounting Framework provides for a systematic and detailed description of the UK economy. This includes accounts for different, but still highly aggregated, sectors:

- non-financial corporations
- financial corporations
- general government (central and local government)
- households
- non-profit institutions serving households
- the rest of the world.

A more detailed breakdown is given by an 'industrial classification'. The one applied to the collection and publication of a wide range of economic statistics is the Standard Industrial Classification. The current version, SIC92, is consistent with the industrial classification used in the European Union. Later chapters of this book will discuss the market for leisure and tourism and Chapter 8 particularly discusses the use of Standard Industrial Classification. Within economic statistics we will

find information that is relevant to identifiable leisure and tourism-related industries, as well as information setting the overall economic environment within which these industries operate. We will return to this in a later section of this chapter.

Economic transactions between UK residents and the rest of the world are described in greater detail in the 'balance of payments', for which the annual publication is the Pink Book. The balance of payments is another of the UK's key economic statistics. It also draws a series of balances between inward and outward transactions, provides an overall net flow of transactions between UK residents and the rest of the world, and reports how that flow is funded.

Economic transactions included in the balance of payments include:

- exports and imports of goods (such as sports and leisure goods and clothing)
- exports and imports of services (such as international transport used by tourists and for the carriage of goods)
- income flows (such as dividends and interest earned by foreigners on investments in the UK and by the UK investing abroad)
- financial flows (such as direct investment, say by multinational leisure enterprises within the UK), including investment in shares, debt securities, loans and deposits
- transfers, which are offsetting entries in the balance of payments account to any one-sided transactions listed above, such as foreign aid and funds bought by people migrating to the UK.

Social statistics

Social statistics cover a wide range of information about households, families, individuals and the condition of the society in which we live. Social statistics are produced according to standard definitions and use agreed classifications, so that the statistics should be consistent and comparable. The National Statistics socio-economic classification, for example, is used to report survey results for different sections of the population. It is based on the occupation and employment status of the respondent. This classification was introduced for the 2001 Census and for ongoing social surveys with effect from April 2001. It replaces the 'social class' classification used in official statistics.

Social statistics are less structured than economic statistics in that there is no overarching framework for social statistics equivalent to the system of National Accounts. Nevertheless, there is an extensive amount of statistical information covering all the domains of interest to social policy, including the labour market, education and training, health and care, household and family structure and formation, crime and justice, population growth and structure, and migration within the UK and internationally.

An effective system of social statistics would aim to include a wide range of components that together would describe and explain the level of well-being of society as a whole and of the groups and individuals within it. It would also enable changes over time to be monitored and explained. Official statisticians in the UK and in other countries increasingly see social statistics as a system needing a framework analogous to the system of national economic accounts. A framework for social statistics would help to determine priorities for developing statistics, based on an evaluation of gaps and set against the requirements for statistics indicated by the framework.

In summary, social statistics seek to describe the following macro issues:

- the number and characteristics of the population at any time or place (including as a result of internal and international migration, as well as from births, deaths, marriages and other household and family changes); these are often seen as the traditional statistics about 'vital events' needed in resource allocation and for policy and operational planning
- the experience within that population of various sub-groups: the old, the young, ethnic minorities, the disabled, women, the unemployed, and so on
- changes in these characteristics and experiences over time.

They also describe the following micro issues:

- inequality of experience at the individual level and how it is changing: income, education, health, victimisation and access to services
- social contribution: interactions between work, volunteering, caring, education, rest and idleness
- multi-dimensionality: how common factors cluster among individuals revealing associations between crime, achievement and place
- social mobility: trajectories, lifetime pathways, opportunities and risks (including intergenerational links and changes)
- compound issues
- social capital: the value of family, community, networks and cohesiveness.

These aspects are listed above in increasing levels of complexity. The priority requirement for the relatively new development of 'neighbourhood statistics' (including to inform and evaluate policies of neighbourhood renewal) is at the simpler, macro end of the spectrum. Social statistics as a whole seeks to develop across the whole spectrum. And, of course, the different levels help to inform development and understanding of each other. For example, analysis in the 'social contribution' area may suggest new indicators of the 'characteristics' of the population. Similarly, changes in the 'characteristics' of the population such as an increase in single parent families will inform analysis of inequalities between different types of family.

The framework that is emerging to describe the range of social statistics is illustrated in Figure 2.1. In the framework we can see how the requirements of a system of social statistics fit together. The left-hand part describes the characteristics of interest, the centre box the various sub-groups of the population of interest, the right-hand box dimensions of change over time and differences between areas. The contextual and infrastructure parts of the system are important when looking at the more complex issues of explaining inequalities and multi-dimensionality.

The information requirements that follow from such a framework for social statistics cover a wide range, especially when including the wider macro-economic,

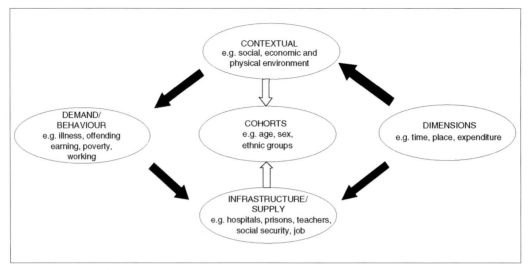

Figure 2.1   Framework for social statistics

social and physical environment. This reflects the understanding that the different layers of influence do not operate in isolation but interact in complex relationships. Within the broad range, specific domains of information needed to be identified and defined. This is primarily to reflect the main social policy areas, such as education, crime and the labour market, but also aids the planned acquisition and organisation of data. Adding specific domains into the picture can be summarised by the diagram in Figure 2.2.

Figure 2.2 is derived from the domains of interest identified in work to form the basis for better statistical information for neighbourhood renewal. It applies more generally across social statistics. At the centre of any statistical system is information about the number and characteristics of the population that live in the area of interest, whether this is the UK as a whole or a nation, region, local area or neighbourhood within the UK. There is increasing interest in including ethnicity as a population characteristic. Then six domains of socio-economic circumstances that feature commonly in descriptions of deprivation or social exclusion are identified. These are: work, education, housing, health, crime

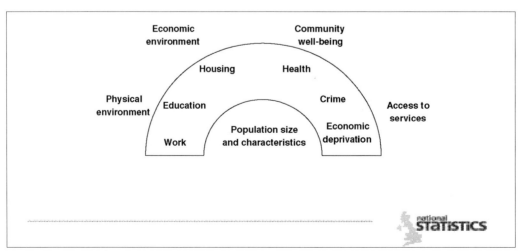

Figure 2.2   Framework for social statistics by subject and domain

and economic deprivation. These factors describe the circumstances of people and families and can be aggregated to describe neighbourhoods or other areas. They also often relate to one another, so that, for example, educational attainment, health and labour force participation are intertwined. The final four domains identified in Figure 2.2 are the physical environment, the economic environment, community well-being (also seen as 'social environment') and access to services.

Having set out a framework, the task is then to work out what statistical information is needed within each domain. This is determined by the availability of existing statistics and by interactions with the users and producers of statistics. Academic work, for example on social exclusion and on sustainable development, will also inform this process. In the example in Figure 2.3, we look at possible statistical needs to help understand crime. In the centre is the population of interest, in this case, the perpetrators and victims of crime or the people who live in fear of crime. These characteristics will be related to age and sex and possibly other factors such as ethnicity. We will be interested in aspects of crime such as the time of day, week or year that the crime took place, and look at trends from year to year, as well as what happens to people involved in crime during the course of their lives. The spatial distribution of crime will also be of interest, as will be society's expenditure on crime prevention, control and its

social costs. These are all represented in the 'dimensions' part of the framework.

The model for social statistics that we have been illustrating here is based on a generalised supply and demand, quasi-economic model. In the example of Figure 2.3, 'demand' is characterised by behaviour – crime – or behaviours resulting in fear of crime, or behaviours characteristic of victims. We need to know as much as possible about this aspect of crime. In reaction to this 'demand' is society's 'supply'. In this case the provision of prison, probation, police and crime prevention services, as well as the activities of the criminal justice system in the law and courts. At the top of the model are the contextual factors such as health and education. We could also add employment, leisure and other related social policy areas. Indeed, Chapter 4 makes use of such household characteristics to help to explain participation in sports. Infrastructure factors, physical and social environments also fit in to this part of the model. So, for example, a housing estate with lots of dark alleyways and landings and a low level of social cohesion is likely to experience high levels of crime and even to produce its own criminals and population with high levels of fear of crime.

We have gone into this example in some detail both to illustrate how the model works and to indicate how it can be developed in other social policy areas,

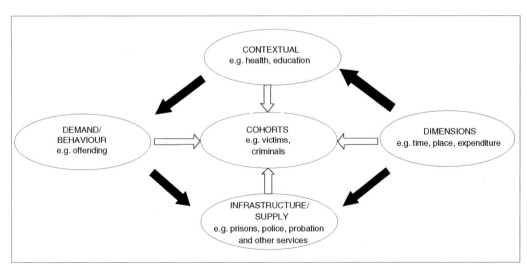

Figure 2.3 Framework for social statistics relating to crime

such as health or education. For example, there is little point in knowing all about what goes on in the health service 'infrastructure/supply' if little is known about the actual health and health behaviour of the population. It may be the case that 'supply' increases but has no impact at all on the actual health status of the population, which is really the subject of interest.

Environmental statistics and sustainable development

In recent years, concern about the environment has increased and there is increasing awareness of the need for development that is sustainable. The UK Government's vision for sustainable development is that there is:

- social progress that recognises the needs of everyone
- effective protection of the environment
- prudent use of natural resources
- maintenance of high and stable levels of economic growth and employment.

A wise growth strategy within the overall vision for sustainable development seeks to balance:

- economic growth
- environmental benefits and impacts from tourism
- social benefits (with benefits spread throughout society) and impacts from tourism.

These components of sustainable development are being monitored through a series of sustainable development indicators that are now National Statistics under the general heading of 'quality of life counts'. There is a core set of about 150 indicators of sustainable development, with a subset of 15 'headline' indicators. The UK indicators of sustainable development and other information and publications about sustainable development, are available on the website www.sustainable-development.gov.uk/.

The headline indicators are intended to raise public awareness and focus public attention on what sustainable development means, and to give a broad overview of whether we are achieving a 'better quality of life for everyone, now and for future generations to come'.

Regional versions of the national 'headline' indicators of sustainable development have also been published. In England, a range of initiatives under the Modernising Local Government agenda directly support sustainable development by focusing on the integration of social, economic and environmental issues at the local level. They also encourage greater community participation, and the principle of putting people first. Part 1 of the Local Government Act 2000 places a duty on principal local authorities to prepare 'community strategies', for promoting or improving the economic, social and environmental well-being of their areas, and contributing to the achievement of sustainable development in the UK. A community strategy must have arrangements for monitoring the implementation of the action plan and for reporting progress to local communities. In 2000 the Department of the Environment, Transport and the Regions (DETR) – now the Department for Environment, Food and Rural Affairs (DEFRA) – published a handbook for a menu of 29 local indicators of sustainable development. Further details are at http://www.sustainable-development.gov.uk/indicators/local/index.htm. Although the statistics that result from local applications of this guidance are not included in National Statistics, this is a good example of the connection that may need to be made between National Statistics and more local data sources. This connection is particularly strong in the case of the development of neighbourhood statistics.

Overview of data sources and data collection

The producers of National Statistics get their data from two main sources:

- administrative systems within government
- statistical surveys of households, individuals or businesses carried out in order to produce National Statistics.

Examples of administrative systems used include the UK's trade in goods with non-EC countries, the Inland Revenue's systems for PAYE and taxation of company profits, and the numbers claiming unemployment benefit and social security benefits. Data such as these are relatively cheap and timely to use in statistical outputs. However, they are governed by administrative rather than statistical needs. This means that changes in the working of the system, such as changes in the entitlement to a social security benefit, can lead to discontinuities in the statistical series. However, because of the large quantities of administrative data available, these sources do have powerful applications. For example, the large volumes of information on the claimant count provide a wealth of detail on the age and gender of those claiming unemployment benefit in local areas across the country.

Many statistical surveys are carried out to produce National Statistics. These include the Labour Force Survey and the Retail Sales Inquiry. Surveys of people, businesses or other organisations are designed specifically to give relevant and reliable statistics and to provide a snapshot of a topic at any one particular time. The decennial censuses of population and housing are like a super survey in which everyone in the country is required to reply (rather than being a sample of respondents invited to take part).

Making survey data usable

By the time survey data are published in their final form – giving information on, say, average earnings in each industry – the data will have gone through a number of processing stages. The flow chart in Box 2.3 provides a simplified summary of the main stages involved in the collection, processing and publication of survey data.

Making administrative data usable

Like survey data, data obtained from an administrative system are also likely to require processing before they are ready to publish. In the main, the process is likely to begin by making any necessary adjustments required to bring the concept into line. For example, when they become available, data from the Inland Revenue are used to update much of the annual information on incomes in the National Accounts. However, for the Inland Revenue's taxation purposes, an individual's income figure will exclude any pension contributions that are not taxable as well as excluding all other income earned by someone whose income falls below the tax threshold. For National Accounts purposes,

---

Box 2.3

The stages of processing survey data

Stage 1: Understand the requirement and design the survey form, questions, notes and definitions. Explore use of standard or harmonised questions and concepts. Cognitive testing of individual questions or terms may be necessary (to see how respondents interpret the words used).

Stage 2: Define the population, design and make a sample selection.

Stage 3: Collect the raw data, input them and check them.

Stage 4: Process and gross data to represent the full population.

Stage 5: Aggregate data into categories and variables (with further checking).

Stage 6: Analyse and publish, including for social surveys depositing a dataset of anonymised records in the UK Data Archive.

---

estimates for the pension contributions and those earning below the tax threshold need to be added in.

Administrative data are then likely to proceed through similar aggregation, checking and publication processes as for survey data above. In fact, within the National Accounts, information is likely to be brought together from administrative and from survey sources at the aggregation stage.

Seasonal adjustment

Any analysis of time series data will involve an examination of a general pattern of the data, the long-term movements within the series, and whether there were any unusual circumstances – such as strikes or bad weather – that may have affected the data. However, this type of analysis is not easy using raw time series data, because there may be short-term effects associated with the time of the year that will obscure other (possibly interesting) movements in the series. For example, retail sales go up in December because of the effect of Christmas. Seasonal adjustment is the process used to identify and remove the seasonal component from a time series, allowing a more meaningful comparison of consecutive months or quarters.

In the presentation of many economic series, the emphasis is placed on the seasonally adjusted series. Seasonal adjustment is made in order to give a clearer interpretation of the changes in the final series. At the Office for National Statistics, seasonal adjustment is carried out using a computer package that is essentially a smoothing technique. One of the main aims of the programme is the identification and estimation of the seasonal component. However, seasonally adjusting the components or sub-components of the economic account is not simply a mechanical process. A good knowledge of the series, as well as an understanding of the programme, is crucial in the production of seasonally adjusted series. Moreover, in the tourism sector, for example, seasonality may well be an important issue to model. This is discussed in Chapter 6 when illustrating how to forecast tourism demand.

Data quality

In general, the aim of the producers of National Statistics is to deliver timely, consistent and coherent statistics, which accurately represent activity in the economy and society. Quality is often described as 'fitness for purpose'. Members of national statistical offices across Europe have agreed on seven components by which the quality of official statistics can be measured:

- relevance: concepts, measurements and statistical products reflect user needs
- accuracy
- timeliness and punctuality in disseminating results and responsiveness to user needs on timing
- accessibility and clarity of results: results accessible in a user-friendly manner; users provided with information about quality of the statistics and about methods used to derive the figures
- comparability: allowing reliable comparisons over time and space
- coherence: consistent standards used, so that results from various sources can be drawn on

- completeness: coverage reflecting user needs.

To help users assess the quality of National Statistics, various quality measures are published alongside the statistics. For example, the revisions to growth rates of GDP are published periodically in *Economic Trends*, which helps users assess the accuracy of the statistics and the relevance of the initial publication of the data. This is often less accurate than estimates derived later and with more complete data. Sampling errors, which can be estimated for random samples, are published. The regular quality reviews now undertaken as part of the process to deliver National Statistics provide opportunities to assess the quality of sets of statistics and to consider how the various dimensions of quality might be improved where necessary.

Where does leisure and tourism fit within National Statistics?

We have seen that National Statistics provide information setting the overall economic, social and environment context, within which leisure and tourism takes place. Tourism is mentioned explicitly in the title of one of the themes within National Statistics, along with transport and travel, while leisure is covered by the social and welfare theme. At present there are not many National Statistics products dedicated to leisure or tourism, although various sets of statistics can be drawn together from National Statistics products and databases in order to build a picture of leisure and tourism. Statistics on tourism published by the national tourist boards are not, at the time of writing, part of National Statistics.

On the supply side, a group of industries have by convention become known as the 'tourism-related industries' because the group of industries is believed to account for a significant proportion of tourism spending. The group also covers a number of leisure activities as well. The industries are listed in Table 2.1, as indicated by their Standard Industrial Classification (SIC) category and illustrated with statistics on the employment in the industries. Other statistics that could be obtained are, for example, the turnover of businesses in this industry group, or average earnings in each industry.

An example of how this would work is given in the journal *Cultural Trends* (Allin, 1998). The author defined the film and video sector of the economy in terms of three relevant categories within the Standard Industrial Classification (SIC codes 92.11, 92.12 and 92.13, which cover motion picture and video production, distribution and projection respectively). The author was able to extract National Statistics on the number of businesses in these categories, the total workforce employed, the turnover of the businesses, their exports, imports and trade balance, the value added by these industries and their net capital expenditure. Also, one of the items recorded and published in the National Statistics *Expenditure and Food Survey* (EFS) is household spending on cinema admissions. The ONS uses the EFS and other data to construct a quarterly series of consumer expenditure on cinema admissions. All of this provided a comprehensive statistical description of the film and video sector. However, it meant going to a number of different sources. Data varied in how current they were.

Users whose interest in tourism and leisure statistics is mainly about international transactions between the UK and overseas will find some relevant statistics published as part of the balance of payments. The 'travel account' within the balance of payments records expenditure within the UK by visitors, and by UK visitors abroad; it covers the following categories:

- business expenditure by seasonal and border workers
- other expenditure by business travellers
- expenditure by non-business travellers (including travel related to health and education, as well as holidays, visits to friends and relatives and other personal international travel and tourism).

A section on 'personal, cultural and recreational services' in the balance of payments is divided into audiovisual and related services and 'other'. The first category, audiovisual and related services, covers services and associated fees relating to the production of motion pictures (on film or video tape), radio and television programmes (live or on tape) and musical recordings. It includes rentals, fees received by actors, directors, producers and so on.

The second category covers all other personal, cultural and recreational services, including those associated with museums, libraries, archives, provision of correspondence courses by teachers or

Table 2.1   Employment in tourism-related industries in Great Britain, September 2001

Industry	SIC category	Number of jobs
Hotels and other tourist accommodation	551 and 552	410,900
Restaurants, cafés etc.	553	556,200
Bars, public houses and nightclubs	554	528,000
Travel agencies and tour operators	633	140,900
Libraries, museums and other cultural activities	925	81,800
Sport and other recreational activities	926 and 927	414,600
All tourism-related industries		2,132,400
Of which:		
employee jobs		1,955,800
self-employment jobs		176,600

Source: ONS (2002) *Labour Market Trends*, Table B17

doctors, and so on. Income received directly from abroad by examining bodies and correspondence course colleges is also included.

Within social statistics we will find much information that is relevant to the leisure and tourism activities of people and households. For example, social statistics provide information about the population overall and so can be analysed within the catchment areas of leisure and tourism facilities. We can see how population changes over time by using the mid-year population estimates and population projections. The decennial censuses of population and ongoing surveys provide statistics on the demographic characteristics of residents and visitors to the UK, such as sex, age range and ethnic group. Censuses have been conducted every ten years. Results from the Census of Population 2001 were published during 2002 and 2003 and provide a wealth of statistical information, down to small geographic areas.

The latest international development of the system of national accounts included the proposal that various 'satellite accounts' should be produced, to supplement the traditional presentation of national accounts. Of particular interest is the concept of a tourism satellite account (TSA). A TSA provides a means of separating and examining tourism supply and tourism demand within the general framework of the system of national accounts. The conventional national accounts of a country do not routinely distinguish tourism as a separate activity. This is because tourism is essentially a 'demand side' activity. People become tourists for a period of time and then they return home. Many businesses serve tourists but they also serve other customers.

The methodological design of a standard tourism satellite account has been proposed jointly by three international organisations (the World Tourism Organisation, the Organisation for Economic Co-operation and Development, and the Statistical Office of the European Communities). The design was approved in 2000 by the United Nations Statistics Commission. A number of countries are developing tourism satellite accounts and a study within the UK has shown that it would be feasible to produce a tourism satellite account here. At the time of writing, no decision had been reached on whether or not to produce such an account.

Further information on tourism satellite accounts is available on the websites of the World Tourism Organisation (www.world-tourism.org) and of the OECD (www.oecd.org).

Conclusion

The set of National Statistics is evolving and is already a major source of authoritative statistics on the economy, society and the environment. There is free access to all National Statistics for all users, via the National Statistics website (as long as the information downloaded is not intended for commercial use, in which case a licence and a fee has to be agreed). A series of developments is set out in the National Statistics work programme.

Leisure and tourism are within the scope of National Statistics. A range of information can be extracted from them that is relevant to particular leisure and tourism activities and more generally to the environment in which they operate. Subsequent chapters of this book give an illustration of how these statistics might be employed to aid decision-making. However, there is potential for more data on leisure and tourism to be included in the set of National Statistics, for example the production of a tourism satellite account in order to determine the contribution of tourism to the economy, if this would meet user needs.

Resources

The following regular publications are produced by the Office for National Statistics and published by Palgrave Macmillan, with the exception of Transport Statistics GB, which is produced by the DETR and published by The Stationery Office (London).

• United Kingdom National Accounts: The Blue Book (annual)
• United Kingdom Balance of Payments: The Pink Book (annual)
• Social Trends (annual)
• Consumer Trends (quarterly)
• Economic Trends (monthly)

- Travel Trends – A Report on the International Passenger Survey (annual)
- Transport Statistics GB (annual)
- Family Spending: Report on the Expenditure and Food Survey (annual)
- Living in Britain: Results from the General Household Survey (annual; web only from December 2004).

These and many other publications – including the Census of Population 2001 and UK Time Use Survey – are also available on the National Statistics website. Further information is available in the *National Statistics Guide to Products and Services* (2005 edition forthcoming), available from the National Statistics Customer Contact Centre, which is a comprehensive list of all National Statistics products available on the National Statistics website. See Box 2.1 for contact information.

3 Sources of UK tourism research data

Dr Brian Hay Head of Research, VisitScotland

Focus questions

- Where can I get statistics on the tourism industry?
- How is tourism defined?
- What are the aims of tourism statistics?
- How is tourism measured?

Introduction

Information on tourism statistics is available from an extensive range of surveys and details of the aims, methodology and data availability from the six main tourism surveys are discussed in this chapter. Most of the data are available in either printed form or increasingly through various websites, and details on how to access these surveys are also discussed. In addition, a set of working definitions of measured variables in data sources is provided.

Tourism surveys

The main sources of data on tourism are:

- the International Passenger Survey
- the United Kingdom Tourism Survey
- the British Conference Market Trends Survey
- the United Kingdom Occupancy Survey
- the United Kingdom Attractions Survey
- the Great Britain Day Visits Survey.

The International Passenger Survey

The International Passenger Survey (IPS), which measures the volume and value of overseas tourism to the UK, has been conducted continuously since 1961, and has been gradually extended to include all the main air, sea and tunnel ports or routes into and out of the UK. Routes to and from the Channel Islands, the land boundary with the Irish Republic and cruise ships travelling to or from the UK are excluded, but estimates are made of tourists using these routes. Thus, about 90% of all passengers arriving into or leaving the UK are covered by this survey. The main measurements provided by the IPS are number of visits, spending in sterling and the length of stay in nights, with the main and most useful data analysed by a number of characteristics. These include mode of transport (air, sea or tunnel), parts of the UK visited (country, county or by regional tourist board area), purpose of visit, quarter of visit, age group, gender, length of stay and type of vehicle. For the purpose of the survey, a tourist is defined as someone on a trip of less than one year, and includes day visitors, those on holidays, business, visiting friends and relatives, study trips or travelling to receive medical attention. Migrants, air and ship crews and those do who not disembark are not included in the survey.

Aims and methodology

The IPS is a large multipurpose survey, which collects information from passengers as they enter or leave the United Kingdom. It is conducted by the Office for National Statistics (ONS) and the aims of the survey are:

- to collect data on credits and debits for the travel account of the UK balance of payments
- to provide detailed information about overseas visitors to the UK so as to assist in the formation of tourism policy
- to provide data on international migration
- to collect travel information on passenger routes as an aid to aviation and shipping authorities.

The survey is based on over 260,000 face-to-face interviews per year with passengers travelling to or from all the principal sea and air routes and the Channel Tunnel. The sample is stratified to ensure it is representative by mode of travel (air, sea and tunnel), port or route and time of day, with interviews conducted throughout the year. Not all those surveyed are asked the full set of questions; for example information on spending and length of stay in the UK is sought of only some overseas tourists as they leave the country, as activity actually undertaken while in the UK may differ from that originally planned.

In the 2000 survey, some 57,000 interviews were conducted with overseas visitors as they left the UK and 57,000 with UK residents as they arrived in the UK. The response rates are very good, with 81% of those interviewed in the 2000 survey providing complete or partial responses. The data on sampling errors for the 2000 estimates of overseas visitors at the relative 95% confidence interval are: 3.0% for visits, 3.8% for nights and 2.9% for spend data. The sampling scheme used in this survey is a multi-staged one, which is carried out separately for air, sea and Channel Tunnel travel. Interviews are conducted in all terminals at Heathrow, Gatwick and Manchester airports, with interview shifts designed to cover the expected passenger flows, with every 67th passenger interviewed. Interviews are also conducted at other airports with more than 50,000 international passengers per quarter, at all sea routes with more 50,000 passengers per year, as well as people using the Channel Tunnel.

Access to the results

The monthly results are published in the ONS First Release series 'Overseas Travel and Tourism', and are usually available some two months after the survey period. They can be obtained free of charge from www.statistics.gov.uk/products. Quarterly results of the IPS are published in electronic format in MQ6, *Transport, Travel and Tourism: Overseas Travel and Tourism*; they are also available on www.statistics.gov.uk/products in pdf format. The full annual results in the form of a compact version of the IPS dataset are available on the CD-ROM *Travelpac* at £35+ VAT for the 1993 to 2000 datasets. National Statistics also produces a useful 150 page report annually, *Travel Trends – A Report on the International Passenger Survey* (price £41), which is available from Palgrave Macmillan.

Information is available to varying degrees from the research departments of the national tourist boards. Recent data on overseas tourists to the UK and the regions are also available through the VisitBritain (VB) tourism industry professional site (TIPS) at www.visitbritain.com/corporate, although to make full use of the site you need to apply for a password. It is possible to commission more detailed analysis of the IPS from the marketing agencies appointed by the ONS marketing agencies: Information Research Network (www.im-research.com) or MDS Transmodel (www.mdst.co.uk).

The United Kingdom Tourism Survey

The United Kingdom Tourism Survey (UKTS) is designed to provide complementary data to the IPS on tourism within the UK by UK residents. This survey is jointly sponsored by the four UK tourist boards: VisitBritain (VB), Northern Ireland Tourist Board (NITB), VisitScotland (VS) and Wales Tourist Board (WTB). The survey was first conducted in 1989 and, until 1999, it was based on 70,000 in-home interviews each year with adults, using mainly a random omnibus survey. Because the survey vehicle was discontinued, the 2000 and subsequent surveys are now based on 50,000 telephone interviews each year using random digit dialling from known blocks of residential telephone numbers. This survey is conducted by Millward Brown on behalf of the tourist boards by means of an exclusive *ad hoc* survey. Because of these changes in methodology, comparisons with the pre-2000 data are not possible. Although the UKTS is designed to provide detailed information about tourism trips taken by UK residents in the UK, it also provides data on travel to overseas destinations by country of residence in the UK.

Aims and methodology

The aims of the United Kingdom Tourism Survey are to measure the volume and value of tourism trips taken by UK residents and to collect details about these trips and the people taking such trips. These aims have been expanded to measure:

• tourism by UK residents of any age; although the survey only interviews those aged 16+, it collects details of all adults and children present on such trips

- tourism for any purpose including holidays, visiting friends and relatives, for work or business purposes, conferences and exhibitions or most other purposes; trips that involve temporary residence in an area, hospital admissions or school visits are excluded
- trips away from home for one or more nights up to a maximum of 60 nights; day trips and trips of more than 60 nights are excluded
- tourism to any destination in any country using any type of accommodation, or no accommodation at all.

Thus all trips, no matter for what purpose or destination as long as they involve an overnight stay away from their normal place of residence, are measured by this survey. The data collected in the UKTS include: trip purpose, accommodation, transport, organisation of trip, type of location, gender, month of trip, length of trip, duration of trip, age, socio-economic group, life cycle, incidence of tourism and activities undertaken (main purpose or participated in when on a trip).

The UKTS is conducted continuously throughout the year by telephone interviewing. The survey design is based on a two-stage probability or 'random' sample. The first stage involves the selection of the households, whereby residential telephone numbers are randomly selected using an equal probability of selection method. This selection is based on a database of all known exchange codes allocated for land-based telephone use in the UK, and numbers are selected with equal probability, with the last four numbers randomised and then checked to confirm it is a working number. This ensures the sample is not clustered. The second sample stage is the selection of the individual, who is chosen by interviewing the person in the household with the most recent birthday. Over 50,000 interviews are conducted each year, using computer assisted telephone interviewing (CATI). The data are weighted to ensure consistency with the known demographic characteristics of the UK population. As well as measuring UK residents' tourism within the UK, the survey also contains limited data on tourism trips to overseas destinations, by country of origin within the UK. At the 95% confidence interval, the sampling errors for the UK data are: 1.9% for trips, 2.5% for night and 3.0% for spend.

Access to the results

Annual data are available from *The UK Tourist: Statistics 2002* (£95), but this report only contains data for 2000. Data from the previous year's reports usually also contain information for the previous five years and are available from the offices of the four UK tourist boards. The 2002 report is about 50 pages long and contains a wealth of detailed information on UK residents' tourism to England, Scotland and Wales, as well as the UK as whole. The joint UK tourist boards and Department for Culture, Media and Sport (DCMS) website (www.staruk.org) is a useful source of data, but only contains limited annual data. Separate summary data for each of the home countries are usually available from the four tourist boards, through publications such as *Tourism in Scotland*, which contains summary data in the form of more than 20 tables. Regional data for England are usually published in their regional tourism reports. The Scottish results are available through www.scotexchange.net, which provides summary reports by region and market segments, such as walking holidays, golfing holidays, business tourism and so on. All four boards hold the annual and monthly data in printed form and through a computer database. Access to these databases varies according to the boards' own policies, but all may be viewed at the boards' offices and, subject to staffing constraints, further data analysis may be possible, possibly with a charge for complex data analysis.

The boards have different policies about releasing in-year data for their country; for example VisitScotland releases limited data on www.scotexchange.net through its monthly report on the year to date. The data are also summarised in the UK Trends Reports, which each year cover the periods January to April, and January to June, July, August and September, respectively; they are available about three months after the survey month. These reports contain weighted data by type of trip by destination or origin country of trip within the UK, and on overseas trips by UK residents, but access to these reports is dependent on individual boards' policies.

The British Conference Market Trends Survey

In order to measure the importance and the value of the conference market in the UK better, since 1994 the British Conference Market Trends Survey (BCMTS) has been conducted every year with only limited changes in the methodology it uses. It is conducted by NFO System Three and is jointly funded by VB, WTB, NITB, VS, International Congress & Conventions Association (ICCA) and the British Association of Conference Destinations (BACD).

Aims and methodology

The aims of the British Conference Market Trends Survey are:

- to measure trends in venue booking and venue choice, size of conferences and other key variables, to provide a reliable measure of the volume and value of conference business tourism in the UK
- to provide a clear picture of the economic benefits of the conference sector to Britain and the various national and regional areas.

A self-completion postal (and from 2001 email) questionnaire is sent at the beginning of each year to some 1,300 conference venues throughout the UK with the purpose of collecting data on conferences that are held on these sites. It is estimated that there are 5,640 conferences venues in the UK, and the survey provides details of the distribution of them by location and venue type. For the purposes of the survey, a conference is defined as 'an out of office meeting of at least six hours' duration involving a minimum of eight people'. The survey provides details not only of the overall size of the market but also about the following variables: residential and non-residential conferences; conference size; month; type (academic, political and so on); start day; overseas and UK delegates; associated exhibition; and delegate rates. The data are also provided by venue type: purpose-built venues, rural hotels, urban or airport hotels, educational establishments, residential centres and multipurpose venues, and for each of the four UK home countries.

Access to the results

The annual report on the BCMTS costs £125 and is available direct from the BACD at www.bacd.com.uk. It is also possible to obtain detailed country information from each of the home country tourist boards.

The United Kingdom Occupancy Survey

The four UK tourist boards decided that the most appropriate way to comply with one of the requirements of the 1995 EU Directive on Tourism Statistics, whereby they had to provide accommodation occupancy rates for 'hotels or similar establishments', would be for each board (or regional board in England) to conduct the various occupancy surveys to an agreed standard.

This methodology is outlined in a manual from which the United Kingdom Occupancy Survey (UKOS) was developed. For the purpose of this survey, hotels were defined as 'hotels, motels, motor lodges, inns, apartments and other similar establishments that provide accommodation for tourists, are arranged in rooms and provide bed-making and cleaning services'. As the EU also required occupancy data not only on hotels but also on 'similar establishments' these were taken to include 'guest houses, farm houses, and bed and breakfast establishments, the latter includes private houses offering accommodation to paying guests where bed-making and cleaning services are provided' but the survey does not include youth hostels or university accommodation.

Aims and methodology

The aim of the United Kingdom Occupancy Survey is:

- to measure the monthly and annual stock use of serviced accommodation in the UK.

Although the survey provides occupancy data for the serviced accommodation sector as whole, separate occupancy data are also available for hotels, guesthouses and B&Bs. The survey collects data about the survey population as well, such as the total number of all known serviced accommodation establishments and bed spaces, the months they are open, profile information about the establishments (number of bedrooms, type of location, membership of a group) and so on. The data collected each month includes the overall number of new guests (UK and overseas), the total number of guests, the total number of bedrooms occupied each night, the maximum number of available bedrooms and the maximum charge per person per night for bed and breakfast. The survey is conducted each month with a representative sample from each of these types of accommodation in each of the survey areas; in 2000, the recruited sample was 7,000 establishments per month, with an analytical sample of 4,000 per month. The data are analysed by the following categories: type of establishment (hotel, guesthouse or bed and breakfast), size of establishment (from 1 to 3 rooms through to 101 or more rooms), tariff (from less than £20 to more than £60 per night) and type of location (seaside or city, and so on). The data are weighted at regional and UK level, so it is representative of the universe by either number of establishments within selected areas and size bands, number of bed spaces within selected areas and size bands or number of rooms within selected areas and size bands. The minimum analytical size for each of the regions (and Wales, Scotland and Northern Ireland) is 200, with 300 as the target sample. The survey covers all known serviced accommodation in a region, that is accommodation both in and out of the boards' various quality assurance schemes. Some of the tourist boards also conduct occupancy surveys for other sectors, such as self-catering or hostels. The sampling error at the UK level is estimated to be 3%, although since the sample is self-selecting rather than random, it is not possible to be absolutely sure of the size of the sampling error.

Access to the results

In order to comply with the EU Directive on Tourism Statistics each month the top line data on occupancy levels are sent to the EU. The tourist boards also produce an UKOS annual report (£40), but of much more use is the annual summary (£25), which contains five-year trend data both by type of accommodation (hotels, guesthouses and B&Bs) and by country within the UK. A monthly summary report with the UK, England, Scotland, Wales and Northern Ireland data is also produced. Three of the boards (Scotland, Wales and Northern Ireland) and many of the regional boards in England also produce monthly summary reports for their areas and provide detailed analytical information on the sectors' performance by type of accommodation, and by the variables previously listed such as tariff bands. They also break down the data by membership of the various quality assurance schemes and by sub-districts of the geographical regions within their area. All the boards also produce an annual written summary report for the various occupancy surveys covering their areas, which provides data on the current year and limited data on previous years. VisitScotland also conducts separate monthly surveys of occupancy levels of hostels, self-catering and touring camping and caravan parks; the full set of all the monthly summaries is available from VisitScotland at £50 per year.

The United Kingdom Attractions Survey

The four UK boards while each conducting their own survey of attendance at visitor attractions in their country also share their data through two publications: *Visits to Tourist Attractions in the UK* and *Sightseeing in the UK*. For the purposes of this survey an attraction is defined as:

> a permanently established excursion destination, a primary purpose of which is to allow access for entertainment, interest, or education; rather than being primarily a retail outlet or a venue for sporting, theatrical, or film performance. It must be open to the public without prior booking, for published periods each year, and should be capable of attracting day visitors or tourists as well as local residents. In addition, the attraction must be under a single business, under a single management, so that it is capable of answering economic questions on revenue, employment, and so on, and must be receiving revenue directly from the visitors.

Aims and methodology

The aims of the United Kingdom Attractions Survey are:

- to monitor trends in the UK visitor attraction sector

• to improve wider understanding of the dynamics of the sector.

The findings are used to inform the regional development and planning of the tourism industry, and to enable the operators to benchmark their operation with similar attractions, within their area and across the sector as whole. The survey is conducted by means of self-completed questionnaires, which are sent to all known attractions in the UK at the beginning of each year, meeting the above definition. Each tourist board is responsible for managing the survey in their country. According to the tourist boards there are about 6,800 attractions in the UK that meet the criteria for the definition of an attraction. Because the boards attempt to collect data from all known attractions, this is really a census rather than a survey, so it is not possible to provide sampling errors.

Access to the results

The annual report listing data on visits to all attractions with over 10,000 visits in the UK, *Visits to Tourist Attractions*, is available from all the four boards at a cost of £40. The survey ceased in 2002. This report contains data by category of attraction, visit numbers for the current year and the two previous years, ownership, seasonal opening and by whether entry is charged or free. Separate reports are available for all attractions in Scotland, Wales and Northern Ireland, which cover visits to all attractions in their country irrespective of the number of visits recorded, and provide detailed analysis of trends to attractions in their own country.

At the UK level, more detailed analysis of trends in visits to tourist attractions is published in *Sightseeing in the UK*, which again is published by the four tourist boards and is available at £45 from the any of the boards. This report attempts to analyse the attractions data by some 12 types of attractions such as historic homes and castles, leisure and theme parks, museums and art galleries, wildlife attractions, workplaces and so on. It also breaks down the data by ownership, revenue, revenue generation by category of spend, capital investment, use of training schemes, origin of visitors and proportion of children. The appendix in the report provides a useful listing of the top ten attractions by some 12 types of attractions in the UK. To date, current monthly information on visits to attractions is only provided by VisitScotland and is available through their website www.scotexchange.net and through a monthly summary report.

The Great Britain Day Visits Survey

This survey has changed considerably over its lifetime, which makes it difficult to provide trend data. The survey was first conducted in 1994, then in 1998, and again in 2002, with the results from this survey available in early 2004. This survey is sponsored by a consortium of agencies (British Waterways, Countryside Agency, Countryside Agency for Wales, VB, VS, WTB, DCMS, Environment Agency, Forestry Commission and Scottish Natural Heritage), which shows the wide interest there is in the data from a policy perspective.

Aims and methodology

The aims of the UK Day Visits Survey are to:

• measure the extent of participation in leisure day visits by the adult population and to identify the profile of trip takers and non-trip takers, and to estimate the scale and value of such trips
• provide information on activities undertaken, destinations visited, time spent at these destination, time of trip, method of transport used and party size and composition.

The 2002 survey was designed to produce a sample size of 8,000 interviews, which included 2,000 interviews in Wales and Scotland and at least 400 interviews in each of the government office regions in England. The actual fieldwork was conducted from March 2002 to February 2003. The survey not only included measurements of leisure day trips away from home base, but also covered day trips from a UK holiday base. The data will be available for all non-regular leisure day trips, as well as leisure day trips lasting three hours or more that were not made regularly. The variables covered by the survey include: location of trip, distance travelled, transport used, party size, age spend by category of spend, party composition and activities undertaken, and the standard details of the respondents such as gender, working status, ethnic background and working status occupation of wage earner.

Access to the results

The 2002 data (which was not yet available in summer 2003) should be presented in a number of forms, including country reports, annual reports and summary reports. The 1998 data are available in the form of a popular summary leaflet, a full annual report (£50) and a 40 page summary report (£15). The Scottish data are available by the 11 main regions in Scotland. Copies of the 1998 full and summary reports are available from the Countryside Agency on www.countryside.gov.uk.

Defining tourism and leisure activity

As well as gaining access to data, researchers should be careful to check the definitions of measured variables in data sources. In this concluding section key definitions are provided. These are working definitions agreed by the UK tourist boards and are used in the surveys described in this chapter.

Definitions

- An *attraction* is 'a permanently established excursion destination, a primary purpose of which is to allow access for entertainment, interest, or education, rather than being primarily a retail outlet or a venue for sporting, theatrical, or film performance. It must be open to the public without prior booking, for published periods each year, and should be capable of attracting day visitors or tourists as well as local residents. In addition, the attraction must be a single business, under a single management, so that it is capable of answering economic questions on revenue, employment, and so on, and must be receiving revenue directly from the visitors.

- A *tourist* is 'someone staying overnight from their normal place of residence for the purpose of pleasure, leisure, holiday, business (including attending meetings, conferences, exhibitions, incentive travel), visiting friends and relatives or any other non permanent stay'.

- A *conference* is 'an out of office meeting of at least six hours' duration involving a minimum of eight people'.

- A *day trip* is 'a trip for non regular leisure purposes which does not involve an overnight stay away from home'.

- A *tourist day trip* is 'a trip for non regular leisure purposes lasting three hours or more but does not involve an overnight stay away from home or a holiday base'.

- A *hotel* is 'a place charging for guests staying overnight and offers bed making and cleaning facilities, as well as breakfast and evening meals, and has the ability to sell alcohol to both residential and non-residential guests'.

- A *bed and breakfast establishment* is 'a private home which offers rooms for let at a charge and provides a bed making and cleaning service and offers a breakfast which is included in the daily charge'.

- A *guesthouse* is 'a private home which offers rooms for let at a charge and provides a bed making and cleaning service and offers a breakfast which is included in the daily charge, and normally offers an evening meal'.

Publications

Box 3.1

British Conference Market Trends Survey 2001. NFO System Three, Edinburgh. British Tourism Authority, English Tourism Council, Northern Ireland Tourist Board, VisitScotland, Wales Tourist Board, British Association of Conference Destinations, International Congress & Convention Association, Meetings Industry Association

Leisure Day Visits: a Report of the 1998 UK Day Visits Survey. National Centre for Social Research, London. Countryside Agency. ISBN 0 86170 607 2

Visits to Visitor Attractions 2002. Moffat Centre for Travel and Tourism Development, Glasgow Caledonian University. VisitBritain, Northern Ireland Tourist board, VisitScotland, Wales Tourist Board. ISBN 0 86143 297 7

Sightseeing in the UK 2000. Moffat Centre for Travel and Tourism Development, Glasgow Caledonian University, Glasgow. English Tourism Council, Northern Ireland Tourist Board, VisitScotland, Wales Tourist Board. ISBN 0 86143 292 4

Tourism Statistics: International Perspectives and Current Issues. Continuum, London. Edited by J J Lennon, 2001. ISBN 0 8264 5075 X

Travel Trends – A Report on the 2001 International Passenger Survey. The Stationery Office, London. November 2002. ISSN 1360-5895

UK Occupancy Survey for Serviced Accommodation: 2002 Summary of Results. Centre for Leisure Research, Edinburgh. English Tourism Council, Northern Ireland Tourist Board, VisitScotland, Wales Tourist Board. ISBN 0 86143 257 6

The UK Tourist: Statistics 2002. VisitBritain, Northern Ireland Tourist Board, VisitScotland, Wales Tourist Board. ISBN 0 7095 7784 2

Further information on all the publications listed is available from the research departments:

VisitBritain, Thames Tower, Black's Road, London W6 9EL

Northern Ireland Tourism Board, St Anne's Court, 59 North Street, Belfast BT1 1NB

VisitScotland, 23 Ravelston Terrace, Edinburgh EH4 3TP

Wales Tourist Board, Brunel House, 2 Fitzalan Road, Cardiff, CF2 1UY

Part II

Demand in sports, leisure and tourism

4 Understanding participation in sports, leisure and tourism

Dr Paul Downward Institute of Sport and Leisure Policy, Loughborough University

Focus questions

- Why is participation in sports, leisure and tourism relevant to business decisions?
- How can consumer tastes be proxied?
- Are sports, leisure and tourism demands hierarchical?
- How can participation be measured?
- What is derived demand?
- How can participation be modelled?
- What determines the consumption of time?

Introduction

Previous chapters have analysed the broad sources of data that may be employed in aiding business decision-making in the sports, leisure and tourism sectors. In this chapter attention turns towards producing an understanding of the consumer's decision to participate in sports, leisure and tourism activities. The chapter aims to produce a general framework within which one can understand the demand for sports, leisure and tourism. Subsequent chapters exploit this framework by providing extended applications of how official data can be used to explain and forecast demand.

This chapter first of all critically outlines alternative views of the broader structure of demands for sports, leisure and tourism identifying participation as having a central place in this structure. To probe more deeply into this relationship it then outlines how various theories of demand may be related and suggests a common structure of models. The next section then examines conceptual and measurement issues associated with modelling participation. Reference is then made to official data to show how both descriptive and inferential insights on participation can easily be established. The final section shows how official data can be combined with data provided by commercial organisations to provide further understanding of demand. Important caveats are attached to the use of commercially produced data.

The structure of sports, leisure and tourism demand

To begin to understand the complex nature of the structure of sports, leisure and tourism demands it is informative to begin with the proposal that demands are linked hierarchically. This structure follows from elements of basic economic theory and, in particular, 'derived' demand

The concept of derived demand can be traced back to the roots of economic theory and, in particular, Alfred Marshall, who argued that, 'The demand for raw materials and other means of production is *indirect* and is *derived* from the direct demand for those directly serviceably products which they help to produce' (Marshall, 1952, p. 316; italics in original).

Writing at the turn of the 20th century it should be clear to readers that Marshall was not at all concerned with the sports, leisure and tourism industries, but focused attention on the manufacturing and construction sectors of the economy. These were the current engines of growth and seen to be the appropriate focus of analysis. Nonetheless, Marshall's analysis enables us to think carefully about how demands are interlinked in the economic system. In particular in Marshall's schema the demand for, say, a manufactured good lies at the apex of a pyramid from which *derived* demands for inputs followed. Figure 4.1 illustrates the basic ideas using Marshall's original example.

Here, the tastes and preferences of consumers combined with the constraints they face, such as income, produce a demand for housing. In turn the economic system calls forth a demand for 'factors of production' or inputs to produce housing: capital in the form of bricks, plaster and cement; labour in the form of plasterers and builders; and, of course, land on which to build. Based on this idea Marshall proposed that the presence of four main features enabled one to deduce the relationships that would describe this structure. Essentially they focused on how the prices of goods such as housing affect the prices of factors of production.

The relationship between demand and derived demand

- Factors should be essential to the production of the final good or commodity.
- If the final good is inelastic in supply, that is larger relative price increases are needed to call forth a particular relative increase in supply, changes in demand will have a larger affect on its price and thereby make it profitable for contractors to pay more for factors of production.
- A factor should form a small proportion of total costs.
- Reductions in final demand will affect the costs of factors of production implying that the prices of relatively available or substitutable resources will fall faster than prices of more scarce and non-substitutable resources.

Each of these features is independent but their effects can be cumulative. Thus the final three points indicate, for example, that a fall in demand can affect prices, which reduces demands for factors of

production and hence their prices, but the prices of scarce or necessary factors of production will be affected least. It is clear that the relative substitutability in production of factors will govern the differential prices that they can receive.

It is relatively straightforward to apply Marshall's analysis in the sports, leisure and tourism context. Figure 4.2 illustrates the basic structure of demand for sports, leisure and tourism.

Here consumers' tastes and constraints determine a feasible desire to participate in a leisure activity, say, keep fit through 'spinning'. The act of participation thus calls forth a set of derived demands. In the case of spinning there will be a need for equipment, such as exercise bicycles. There will also be a demand for appropriate clothing, for example, cycling shorts, as well as a facility demand, such as room space, sound system and so on. Likewise, the demand to participate in hill walking as a leisure activity will involve a demand, for travel to access the appropriate venue, such as a national park, as well as demands for clothing, footwear and possibly footpaths. Clearly, therefore, this hierarchical structure of demands is a useful organising schema.

There are, of course, complications associated with this simple model. The main one is that it implicitly assumes a one-way causality from participation to demands for equipment and so on. This follows naturally from Marshall's original analysis. In the case of sports and leisure, however, it could be argued that matters are more complicated. For example, it is well known currently that sports clothing has fashion value. This means that the demand for sports clothing can be entirely unrelated

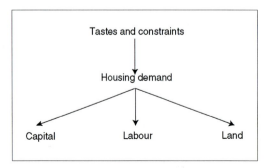

Figure 4.1   Model showing the concept of derived demand

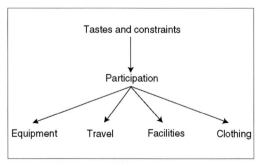

Figure 4.2   Model showing the structure of demand for sports, leisure and tourism

to the level of participation in sports or leisure activities. Likewise this problem arises if one thinks of leisure demands associated with tourism. It may well be that travel is an integral part of the main 'product' rather than a derived demand reflecting the need to travel to consume the tourism product.

This, of course, does not necessarily undermine Marshall's analysis. The problem arises in the above examples because of the varying degrees by which demands are considered to be 'separable' or 'joint' respectively. These are issues of which Marshall was well aware and, in practice, show that the definition of specific markets and products will be of paramount importance. This is, of course, an empirical issue that needs to be determined in particular contexts. Indeed, the above analysis suggests that understanding sports, leisure and tourism demand can be informed with reference to appropriate theory and measurement. In the next two sections of this chapter the theory and appropriate measurement of demand are discussed.

Locating participation within the general theory of demand

The demand for time

It is clear that demand analysis stemming from economic, forecasting or marketing departments or personnel draws on relevant theory either implicitly or explicitly and it is fair to say that economic theory provides the framework within which one can organise this analysis. However, the demand for commodities such as food and drink, clothes, cars and housing, as discussed by Marshall, are typically assumed in economics to reflect the desire to consume material goods.

It is clear, however, that once one introduces sports, leisure and tourism into our considerations then matters are more complicated. These activities are all concerned with the 'consumption' of non-obligated time. As discussed above this raises definitional issues. To reiterate the point, shopping can be seen as a necessary or obligatory economic activity in being the literal process with which we provide goods and services for our consumption. In contrast, shopping can also be viewed as a leisure activity embracing

social intercourse and non-essential activity. We discuss these matters empirically, below. In a theoretical sense the most pressing issue is the question of how we can understand how individuals allocate their time between obligations and sports and leisure activities. The income–leisure trade-off model provides a rudimentary foundation on which the analyst can explore the demand for time.

As Chapter 2 argues, the structure of the economic system – known as the circular flow of income – implies that economic activity involves households comprising individuals who consume products but who also provide work effort for firms to produce things. Basically, in order to consume the household needs to work to earn income. Herein lies a dilemma for the household or individual. The consumer–producer likes both income and leisure. The former is to provide sufficient resources to buy things, including leisure items that the consumer will enjoy. The latter is desirable as an activity in itself. However, because there is a time limit on the individual's capacity to work or to enjoy leisure (and indeed consumption generally) this implies a trade-off. Can we understand this trade-off in more detail? The neoclassical economist, drawing on the analytical apparatus of Marshall, provides an answer in terms of a model of individual rational choice.

The income–leisure trade-off

Economists have devised a relatively simple model to explore this dilemma and hence represent individual rational choice. It is called the income–leisure trade-off model.

The main assumptions of the model are as follows:

- Individuals seek to maximise their utility in seeking to consume goods and services through the acquisition of income. Alternatively they can enjoy leisure time. Utility is simply defined as 'satisfaction'. It is considered to be a personal phenomenon and is *ordinal* in nature. This means that individuals can compare two situations for themselves only and express a preference over them without being able to say anything about the extent of their preference.
- The consumer–producer always prefers more of both income and leisure to less of both. This

implies that they are both 'normal goods' and that the individual is willing to substitute more of one for less of the other. It follows that if the individual gives up some leisure or income, then to leave the individual feeling as well off as previously, more income or leisure respectively is required. It is also usually assumed that if, for example, the individual was currently consuming a lot of leisure, then it would take a smaller relative increment in income to persuade the individual to decrease their leisure by a certain amount and vice versa. This is known as *diminishing marginal utility*.

- Individuals are constrained in their activities by the rate of pay (per unit of time, for example hour, day or month) and the finite amount of time available in the working period. Thus if the rate of pay is £10 per hour and noting that there are 24 hours in a day, then this means that the individual at the extremes could:
  - not work at all and hence receive no income, but 24 hours of leisure
  - work for 24 hours, and receive an income of £240 but consume no leisure.
- These are, of course, extreme cases and are referred to as corner solutions by economists and it follows that attention is focused on points in between these extremes; thus, the individual could also consume 12 hours of leisure and receive £120 of income, or consume six hours leisure and receive £180 income and so on. The

time constraint thus forces an income constraint given a particular rate of pay.

The simplest way to use this model to analyse leisure demand decisions is to represent the above assumptions on a graph. Figure 4.3 illustrates the income constraint facing consumers, their preferences and the derivation of demands for leisure time and income.

The income constraint

On the vertical axis is a measure of income. On the horizontal axis is a measure of the time period for leisure, for example, 24 hours. The income constraint thus simply plots a straight line from 24 hours leisure and zero income to maximum income and zero leisure.

Individual preferences

These are slightly more difficult to understand. However, if we recognise that individuals would like to obtain more income and leisure then it is clear that the individual's utility must increase as one moves 'north east', so to speak, from the origin of the graph. We also know from the second assumption above that levels of equal utility must correspond to increases in income and decreases in leisure (or vice versa). Thus economists draw 'indifference' curves to represent these assumptions.

Each curve represents all the combinations of

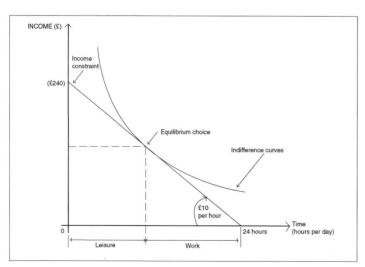

Figure 4.3 The demand for leisure and income

income and leisure yielding a given level of utility. There is a strong analogy here to a contour line on an Ordinance Survey (OS) map. On the OS map contours represent equal heights above sea level. Likewise indifference curves represents alternative combinations of income and leisure with which the consumer feels equally happy.

Two further details are worth noting. The first is that conceptually speaking indifference curves furthest from the origin must indicate increasing utility (rather like climbing an ever-increasing hill! − ever had this feeling?). The second is that the indifference curves are convex towards the origin. The second assumption indicates why this is the case.

Equilibrium choices of income and leisure

Combining the indifference curves and the income constraint enables us to identify qualitatively the individual's rationally defined demands for income and leisure time. The logical point of utility maximisation is where an indifference curve is tangent to the constraint. Moving to the right or left of this point in reallocating leisure and income must force the individual onto a lower level of utility! Technically, this tangency implies that at the optimum combination the consumer will substitute marginal increments of income against leisure at a rate equal to the wage rate. The wage rate thus measures how much value is placed on an hour of time.

Predictions from the model

The above analysis is clearly abstract, somewhat dry and perhaps appears to have no obvious relevance to understanding the demand for leisure. This is certainly true of the model as a description of decision-making. However, the power of the model is revealed in using the model for another role − making predictions. This theoretical objective lies at the core of much economic modelling and, of course, forecasting.

Let's assume that the wage rate increases − wage rates have increased in most advanced economies over time. What are the implications for the demand for leisure? The income–leisure trade-off predicts that two effects will be set in motion.

The substitution effect

As wage rates increase, thinking about the idea of equilibrium, we know that the valuation placed on an hour of time has increased. Basically, it means that the price of leisure has increased. As a normal good this must mean that the demand for leisure will fall and the demand for income through work will rise.

The income effect

On the other hand, it is clear that, as wage rates rise, the same level of work can now purchase more goods anyway. Consequently more of both leisure and income can be achieved. It follows that, for some, more leisure time might be demanded.

It follows that the net effect of these tendencies will produce the new demands for leisure and income. If the substitution effect dominates, less time for leisure will be demanded. If the income effect dominates more leisure will be demanded. Ultimately what happens is dependent on the individual's preferences and is, hence, an empirical question.

In terms of Figure 4.3, one way to illustrate the two effects is by establishing what the new equilibrium point would have been for a particular set of indifference curves − preferences. Figure 4.4 illustrates the changes in demand that occur assuming that the substitution effect dominates. This position has been put forward as applicable for Britain by Gershuny (1996). An increase in the wage rate rotates the income constraint out clockwise around its intercept with the horizontal axis. This is because, while the number of hours in the day remain constant, any extra work now produces more income. This implies that a new tangency will be established on a new indifference curve that also identifies the new demands for income or leisure. As drawn, less leisure time is demanded overall.

Moreover, if we construct a hypothetical income constraint tangent to the original indifference curve but *at a slope corresponding to the new wage rate* this will establish a further hypothetical point of equilibrium on the original indifference curve. The movement from the original equilibrium to the hypothetical equilibrium identifies the substitution effect. The

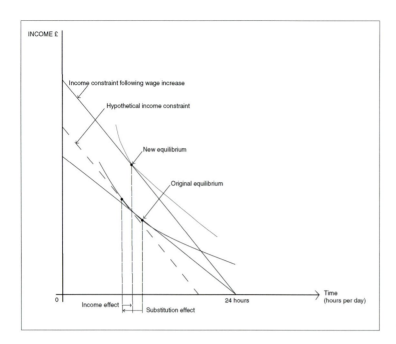

Figure 4.4   The demand for leisure
time following a wage-rate change

movement from the hypothetical equilibrium to the new actual equilibrium identifies the income effect.

Generalising the model

The above sections imply that we have a demand function for leisure time that argues that

$$\text{Leisure time} = F[\text{Wage rate, tastes}]$$

In other words, the demand for leisure time depends on its relative price and consumer preferences. In many respects the simple income–leisure trade-off model is too naïve to provide a good general explanation of demands for sports, leisure or tourism activity. Nonetheless it is relatively easy to generalise.

Theoretical contributions

Theoretical contributions that have helped to generalise the theory of demand have addressed issues associated with the unit of analysis as well as the nature and source of tastes and preferences. In the former case, and essentially extending the neoclassical model, new-household economics associated with, for example, the work of Gary Becker (1976), recognises that individual decisions take place in the household. In taking the idea that individuals are still rational decision-makers, but that they are part of a 'household' unit, Becker argues that the use of time faces competing demands at home. *All non-work activity is not leisure!* Becker's approach thus forces us to think about 'household work' thus generalising the constraint facing individuals. Domestic work like child care, digging the garden, housework and so on are left out of the explanation in the two-way income–leisure trade-off model. The approach has spawned a distinction between *time and goods intensity* in consumption. Some activities consume more time relative to income or goods than others do.

In the latter case, and providing a challenge to the neoclassical and new-household approaches, Tibor Scitovsky (1976) argues that individuals' tastes and preferences are not given. Drawing on psychology he argues that an individual might well seek increased arousal from some decisions and reduced arousal via others, without any presumption of irrationality. Potentially 'sensation seeking', arousal or anxiety is a source of demand for sporting, leisure and tourism activities. In particular this is achieved by balancing boredom and anxiety. Thus whereas the neoclassical model assumes that utility is given, the psychologist recognises that utility is adjusted in line with activities. Consequently, Scitovsky argues that consumption skills need to be learned.

In a similar vein institutional economists argue that consumer choice behaviour and hence tastes are linked to wider social behaviour – in effect through habit and routine. For example in his classic theory of the leisure class, Thorstein Veblen (1925) linked the rise of leisure to the rise in affluence of certain classes following industrialisation. Consequently, Veblen suggests that conspicuous consumption would follow with the desire to demonstrate affluence socially, suggesting that socially defined tastes and income and hence consumption are positively related. Veblen argued that this development was indicative of the decline of the US economy as waste and excess in leisure would begin to permeate the lower strata. There is a clear assumption that productivity would fall. More recently, and generally, critical theory in sociology has attacked attempts to provide sweeping historical generalisations and assumes that behaviour and social life are limited by historical, social and material conditions. Sociologists in this tradition tend to focus on explaining particular problems and situations rather than seeking one universal explanation. They suggest that agreement and coercion can coexist, that shared values and understandings can change and that conflicts can change. Most feminist theories of sports and leisure are critical theories. They would argue that sports are 'gendered' and typically promote 'masculinity' in organised competitive forms. Such theories emphasise that individuals can accept and shape their identities as much as passively respond to them (see, for example, Flintoff and Scratton, 1995; Bramham, 1995).

The implication of these theories is that we can think of demands as having a context outside the simple straitjacket of individual decisions provided by neoclassical economics. In one sense this is absolutely necessary in that the focus for most business decisions is on market demand as opposed to individual demand as, for example, discussed in Chapters 5 and 6. However, the above analysis carries with it the idea that there is more to aggregation than simply adding up demands. It

suggests that one could measure tricky concepts like tastes and social constraints with reference to 'proxies' such as the age, gender and social classes of consumers. While not measuring tastes directly they 'capture' features that will affect them in accordance with the above theoretical arguments.

It is also clear that other factors than simply the price or opportunity cost of sports, leisure or tourism – the wage rate in the income–leisure trade-off model – must figure in a more general theory of demand. Finally, the above analysis also indicates that demands other than participation *per se* need to be accounted for in a general model of demand. Indeed this was implied in the discussion of derived demand. To this end it is possible to offer the following model of sports, leisure and tourism demand that draws on economic theory, yet can be shown to have a direct relevance to these sectors of the economy as demonstrated above. It states that in general demands are a function of relative prices, income and tastes:

$$\text{Quantity demanded} = F[\text{relative price, incomes, tastes}]$$

Empirical contributions

The above statement or function logically suggests how variables are related according to theory and in particular that we would expect the quantity demanded, be it leisure time or, say, a particular piece of sports equipment to vary with its price relative to alternatives, consumer incomes and tastes. The above function is qualitative in that it does not suggest the magnitude of the variations. The direction of the relationship is, of course, implied in the particular theory or set of theories employed to interpret the data in employing the demand function. Thus we might expect a rational individual, or one influenced by the need for 'conspicuous consumption', to increase demand as incomes rise. Likewise, we might hypothesise that the sociological concept of 'masculinity' underpins competitive team sports and as a result this would imply that females have low 'tastes' for these activities relative to males. Consequently data can be analysed descriptively to this end to explore key markets, as illustrated later. Nonetheless, a key feature of official data is that they provide the opportunity to statistically test appropriate demand relationships.

In general demand can be modelled econometrically, by using regression analysis, by postulating the following sort of model:

$$\text{Quantity}_i = \beta_1 + \beta_2 \text{Price}_i + \beta_3 \text{Income}_i$$

Here Quantity is known as the dependent variable, Price and Income are known as the independent variables and 'i' is the set of observations on the variables. $\beta_i (i = 1...3)$ are regression coefficients to be estimated from the data. β_1 is the 'constant' that indicates the average value of demand assuming the other variables were equal to zero. As such, constants often have no obvious and sensible interpretation. The other coefficients indicate the average unit change in the dependent variable following a unit change in the associated independent variable *allowing* for changes in the other variables. The statistical significance of regression coefficients can be assessed to judge whether the measured effects are purely specific to the sample or have general value.

Tastes can be incorporated into the model following the logic of the discussion above by adding variables that measure categories such as individual's sex, ethnicity and so on. Such variables are described as 'dummy variables'. For example, in a sample of data one could score the dummy variable 'sex' as '1' if the individual was a female and '0' if the individual was a male. And include this in the model as illustrated below:

$$\text{Quantity}_i = \beta_1 + \beta_2 \text{Price}_i + \beta_3 \text{Income}_i + \beta_4 \text{Sex}_i$$

Here, β_4 will measure the average deviation in quantity demanded for females compared to males (and vice versa if males were scored '1' and females '0') allowing for the effects of price and income.

Likewise the model is easily transformed to cope with data that perhaps do not come in the form needed to estimate the general demand model. One example would be where one can measure the value of demand as opposed to the physical quantity of demand. The Family Expenditure Survey thus publishes data on the expenditures associated with,

for example, hotels and holidays. Thus in the model

$$(\text{Quantity} \times \text{Price})_i = \alpha_1 + \alpha_2 \text{Income}_i + \alpha_3 \text{Sex}_i$$

α_2 would measure how much expenditure will vary as income varies independently of the sex of the consumer and α_3 would measure how much expenditure varies according to the sex of the individual and independently of their income.

Finally, and of particular relevance to this chapter, the above model can be extended to cases in which demand, as well as variables that proxy tastes, is measured as a categorical value. The General Household Survey (GHS) provides much valuable information on individual and household variables that can be employed to analyse participation. However, participation is measured in a categorical manner. In such circumstances a specialised regression model, known as a logistic model can be employed. It takes the form

$$\text{Log}(P_i / 1 - P_i) = \delta_1 + \delta_2 \text{Income}_i + \delta_3 \text{Sex}_i$$

Here P_i = probability of participating in an activity and $(1 - P_i)$ = the probability of not participating in an activity. $P_i / 1 - P_i$ = the 'odds' of participating in the activity. Consequently, the model can be employed to examine whether or not factors affect the probability of increased or decreased participation. The coefficients in this model thus indicate how much unit changes in independent variables change the log value of the odds ratio, in other words whether or not the likelihood of participation increases.[1] Price is excluded from this example because the GHS does not collect data on prices.

---

1 The log value of the odds ratio appears as the dependent variable for reasons that are beyond the scope of this book. In short the estimation procedure that is used to generate the coefficient values draws on a logistic probability function. This is necessary to produce values of probabilities that lie between '1' and '0'. This is because the dependent variable, which is always assumed to be a random variable in regression analysis, has bounds of '1' and '0' and so the regression analysis tries to predict whether or not observations tend towards either of these values. One needs a specific probability distribution to assess the tendency numerically.

Analysing participation using official data

As noted above, the Office for National Statistics readily publishes data on participation in the GHS for sports and leisure activities, but not for tourism activities. The usefulness of these data is thus demonstrated in the former context.

The GHS is a multipurpose continuous survey carried out by the Social Survey Division of the ONS, which collects information on a range of topics from people living in private households in Great Britain. Based on a stratified random sample of around 15,000 adults it provides a representative picture of the general population. It reports at approximately three-year intervals on sports and leisure participation, most recently in 1993 and 1996 and 2002 (results from which are to be published in 2004). The survey assesses participation for a wide range of sports and leisure activities in two time periods: the last 12 months and the last four weeks. Up to about 1987 only participation in the previous four weeks was assessed. However, this produces the possibility of unrepresentative responses at the individual level because participation could be higher and lower than typical over the year because of seasonal factors. Of course, the reliability of the information is likely to be higher because of the need to remember accurately participation over a shorter period. Combined, therefore, the participation periods provide a reliable source of information.

As well as measuring the participation or otherwise of respondents the GHS also records the frequency of participation. This, of course, adds value to the survey. While the previous section illustrated ways in which the data can be analysed it also alerted the researcher to the need to measure demand in a conceptually correct way. Judgements about this will depend on the context.

Thus simply examining the physical participation in an activity or not indicates nothing about the intensity of the participation or the periodicity of the participation. In an ideal world, to compare like with like, data on all these features should be involved producing an index of demand, for example, that[2]

$$Quantity = Participitation \times Frequency \times Intensity$$

where Participation indicates a number of persons or perhaps the sample proportion who take part in an activity, Frequency measures the number of occasions on which a member of the sampled population took part during some fixed period and Intensity is an index of 'quality' rather than quantity. The latter variable would be difficult to measure. One could use skill levels such as golfing handicaps, but many activities lack these. For instance with walking should the researcher ask participants not only how often they walked and how far but also how much vertical ascent they did, whether there was some scrambling involved, how heavy were the rucksacks, did they simply take their dog to the nearest lamppost![3] There are questions around that attempt to measure intensity, for example, for active sports respondents are asked about whether or not the effort 'was enough to make you out of breath or sweaty' and for walking questions are asked about the speed. However, time pressures in the interview mean that in practice, the GHS concentrates on participation and frequency. Here the benefits of a large sample are balanced against attempts to be over-sophisticated in measurement.

Descriptive analysis

For those interested in quick and easily digested quantitative analysis of participation, the most recent GHS data are presented and analysed in Thomas, et al. (1998) and Fox and Rickards (2004) in which a number of useful tabulations of data appear. Thus, drawing on Thomas, et al. (1998), for example, Table 4.1 presents a comparison of a selection of four activities in terms of their popularity. Such information is important in providing a clear indication of the relative sizes of demands for participation and likely derived demand. This information might be relevant for, for example,

---

2 I am grateful to Alistair Dawson for suggesting this index and raising these issues.

3 It should be noted that in the GHS walking is defined as an activity that must take in a distance of at least two miles.

Table 4.1 Participation in sports and leisure activities, 1996

Activity	Participation rate in 4 weeks before interview	Participation rate in 12 months before interview	Average frequency of participation per participant in 4 weeks before interview	Average frequency of participation per adult per year
Walking	44.5	68.2	*	*
Swimming	14.8	39.6	4	8.2
Keep fit/Yoga	12.3	20.7	7	10.8
Soccer	4.8	8.5	5	3.3
Base = 100%	15,696	15,696		

Source: Thomas, M *et al.* (1998) *Living in Britain: Results from the 1996 General Household Survey*

* Not asked in 1996

those wishing to invest in the provision of sports and leisure facilities, or those wishing to supply sports and leisure equipment. A further important point to note is the sheer size of the sampling exercise, which produces great reliability in the statistics, a factor returned to in the last section of the chapter.

The table illustrates the importance of the GHS's questionnaire strategy as well as the importance of referring to data. In the former case it is instructive to note that participation in all activities differs in participation rates over the year. Thus all participation rates are higher over the past 12 months than the past four weeks and this is particularly the case for swimming. Speculation would suggest that the participation rate for swimming is boosted by holidays, thus reinforcing the need to define demand carefully. In the latter case, despite the apparent importance often attached to soccer, for example, it is quite clear that, of the activities shown, soccer is the least significant in terms of participation. In fact, walking, swimming and keep fit/yoga are the most popular and soccer only ranks seventh overall. These data thus provide valuable insights for the decision-maker into the relative scales of demands for these activities. For example it would appear that the market for swimming facilities considerably outweighs those of soccer pitches. Drawing on the hierarchy of demands argument, moreover, these data suggest

something of the likely level of derived demands that might stem from these activities. Markets in walking boots could be expected to outweigh those in swimming trunks and, say, football boots.[4]

Table 4.2 reports the trends in participation over the decade for the case of respondent replies applicable to 12 months before the interview. The implication is that walking, swimming and keep fit/yoga are broadly speaking growing activities in contrast with soccer. The same might follow then for derived demands.

Thus even if the decision-maker was unsure about extrapolating the relative levels of participation and related demands, the data would suggest that the differences between, say, keep fit/yoga and soccer activities and equipment would increase over time. This accords with our casual experience in noting the widespread growth in private-sector leisure provision.

As well as understanding potential changes in markets overall, as discussed earlier, most theories of participation would draw on factors such as sex, age

---

4 At all times it is taken for granted that the derived demand is genuine and related to participation. Investigation of this issue should always be undertaken. Thus the example refers to football boots as opposed to say replica football kits whose demands are going to be tied in closely with attendance at professional football games rather than participation.

and perhaps (occupational) class as determinants of participation because they proxy tastes and constraints. Regardless of the specific explanation, therefore, knowledge of these impacts on participation enables those making business decisions to understand something of the way in which markets might be segmented (segmentation of the tourist market is discussed further in Chapter 9.) Tables 4.3 and Table 4.4 present participation rates for each of these cases for the four weeks before the interview.

Table 4.3 shows some interesting contrasts. For example, walking and swimming are not strongly linked to sex and participation persists relatively unchanged up to and including ages in the 60s, though participation in swimming drops off quite considerably after 30–34 years of age. This suggests little segmentation in these markets, which conforms to commonsense expectations. In contrast it is clear that soccer and keep fit/yoga have distinct sex-based participation patterns. In essence soccer is a male activity – there are no cases shown for

Table 4.2 Trends in participation in the 12 months before the interview, 1987–1996

Activity	1987	1990	1993	1996
Walking	60	65	65	68
Swimming	35	42	43	40
Keep fit/Yoga	14	19	20	21
Soccer	9	9	8	8
Base = 100%	19,529	17,574	17,552	15,696

Source: Thomas, M et al. (1998) Living in Britain: Results from the 1996 General Household Survey

Table 4.3 Participation according to sex and age in 1996 in the four weeks before the interview

Male activity	16–19	20–24	25–29	30–34	45–59	60–69	>70	Total
Walking	58	58	47	53	52	49	30	49
Swimming	18	17	15	20	9	8	3	13
Keep fit/Yoga	10	10	10	9	5	4	2	7
Soccer	47	28	20	11	2	0	0	9
Base = 100%	418	472	651	1,980	1,729	947	989	7,186
Female activity	**16–19**	**20–24**	**25–29**	**30–34**	**45–59**	**60–69**	**>70**	**Total**
Walking	45	43	44	45	47	41	19	41
Swimming	23	21	24	24	14	10	3	17
Keep fit/Yoga	30	28	25	21	14	11	4	17
Soccer	–	–	–	–	–	–	–	–
Base = 100%	411	567	790	2,392	1,957	1,077	1,316	8,510

Source: Thomas, M et al. (1998) Living in Britain: Results from the 1996 General Household Survey

Table 4.4   Participation according to socio-economic grouping in the four weeks before the interview

Activity	Professional	Employers and managers	Intermediate and junior non-manual	Skilled manual	Semi-skilled manual and personal service	Unskilled manual	Total
Walking	56	48	46	44	39	33	45
Swimming	23	19	17	11	11	6	15
Keep fit/Yoga	14	12	18	7	9	5	12
Soccer	5	4	3	6	3	3	5
Base = 100%	542	2,187	5,091	3,019	2,780	924	15,696

Source: Thomas, M *et al.* (1998) *Living in Britain: Results from the 1996 General Household Survey*

Table 4.5   Participation according to region in the four weeks before the interview

Activity	North	Yorks and Humberside	North West	East Midlands	West Midlands	East Anglia	South East	South West	Great Britain
Walking	41	43	43	44	39	39	46	49	45
Swimming	11	13	14	15	14	16	16	18	15
Keep fit/Yoga	11	12	14	10	12	12	13	12	12
Base = 100%	966	1,362	1,739	1,182	1,456	635	4,629	1,433	15,696

Source: Thomas, M *et al.* (1998) *Living in Britain: Results from the 1996 General Household Survey*

females as the responses were less than 0.5%, which is a protocol adopted by the GHS – and keep fit/yoga a female activity. Derived demands for, say, clothing and equipment are thus likely to be segmented along these lines. Indeed causal experience tells us, for example, that there is a buoyant market in female keep-fit clothing. It is interesting also to note that participation in soccer, particularly, falls off with increasing age. This suggests a young male market. Indeed participation halves over the ten years from leaving school whereas it takes approximately 30 years for the same effect to be felt in keep fit/yoga.[5] Again, this

provides valuable information to the supplier of sports and leisure activities in noting both the need to cater for differences in sex, as well as age, hence scheduling appropriate classes and facilities and so on.

In a similar vein Table 4.4 records participation levels associated with socio-economic groupings.

The results clearly suggest that participation is linked to socio-economic grouping. Higher incomes and perhaps time available to groups other than unskilled manual workers, for example, appears to afford greater opportunities and/or desires to participate. These findings are, of course, consistent with the theoretical ideas discussed earlier. They also suggest that derived demand for sports equipment and so on will be tied to incomes and occupational status. The volume of demand, however, is rooted in middle income groupings. Again, this accords with our casual experience in noting that the growth in

---

5 An implicit assumption being made here is that the cohorts are comparable. So some judgement about this issue needs to be made in a practical context. It is quite clear that tastes might be different between age cohorts because of differences in experience. Drawing on Scitovsky (1976), it might be that older respondents did not get the opportunity to develop tastes for activities that are now much more widely available.

private-sector leisure provision is able to attract subscriptions.

In contrast, Table 4.5 shows in general that participation in the top five activities is not strongly affected by region, though participation in swimming increases as one moves south. This is perhaps to be expected given the likely climate and tourism facilities. Coupled with the data in Table 4.1, Table 4.5 gives the business decision-maker relevant information on which to assess the likely scale of demands in relevant localities.

Thus official data such as the GHS can help the decision-maker to assess the overall growth potential of various interlinked sports and leisure markets as well as to identify key segments in markets of interest qualitatively.

Inferential analysis

Statistical analysis that seeks to test relationships between variables measured in the GHS can be, of course, derived from the raw data as opposed to those already directly presented by the ONS. To illustrate this point the following relatively simple logistic model has been applied to the 1996 GHS data:[6]

$$Log(P_i/1-P_i) = \delta_1 + \delta_2\ Income_i + \delta_3 Sex_i + \delta_4 Age_i$$

As well as the variables noted in the discussion of the model earlier, the age of the respondent has been included to allow some comparisons with the descriptive analysis above. Income is measured in annual equivalent values. Sex is scored '0' for males and '1' for females. Age is measured in years. Table 4.6 presents the results of the analysis for each activity. The first column describes the independent variables applied to the model for each activity. The

6 Data are readily available from the ESRC data archive. Modelling with the data, however, requires some expertise in matching relevant tables from the database. I am grateful to Kevin Macken from the IT department of Staffordshire University Business School for help in this regard. The binary logistic regression model can be estimated within a wide variety of dedicated econometric packages. The widely used SPSS package also includes this facility and was used in this example. A fuller version of this analysis is to be published by Downward, P M (2004).

Table 4.6 Testing the significance of factors determining participation in sports

Walking	Estimated coefficient	Significance level
Income	−0.000004	0.3458
Sex	−0.2323	0.0002
Age	0.0079	0.001
Responses predicted correctly (%)	62.29	

Swimming	Estimated coefficient	Significance level
Income	0.00004	0.0000
Sex	0.5437	0.0000
Age	−0.0209	0.0000
Responses predicted correctly (%)	80.74	

Keep fit/Yoga	Estimated coefficient	Significance level
Income	0.000035	0.0000
Sex	1.2708	0.0000
Age	−0.0327	0.0000
Responses predicted correctly (%)	83.59	

Soccer	Estimated coefficient	Significance level
Income	−0.000007	0.4303
Sex	−3.4403	0.0000
Age	−0.0945	0.0000
Responses predicted correctly (%)	92.79	

Source: GHS (1996)

second column presents the estimated coefficients that describe how a unit change in the independent variable affects the log odds of the respondents participating in the activity.

The final column presents the significance at which the null hypothesis that the estimated coefficient is equal to zero, indicating that the number estimated is chance only, can be rejected. In general, statistical analysis seeks to reject an 'unwanted' hypothesis – known as the null hypothesis. In this case a value for the coefficient equal to zero would imply that the particular variable, to which it is attached, has no effect on participation. The reason for wanting to reject the null hypothesis is because statistical testing requires making a statement about a population coefficient that, by definition, is unknown. Thus one needs to make a hypothesis about its value. Once this is the case then the appropriate statistical distribution can be referred to, to describe the distribution of sample values of the coefficient around the 'true' value. One is then able to make a probability statement about the proximity of the sample value to the population value. Rejecting the null hypothesis means addressing whether or not the chance of the sample value coming from a distribution of values around the true population value is below some small level, say 5%. In statistical language this describes the chance of making a type-1 error: rejecting a null hypothesis when it is true.[7] The final row in the case of each activity records the degree to which the estimated model predicts the behaviour of the respondents, that is whether or not they participate in the activity. It is a measure of the 'goodness of fit' of the model. Other measures are available but they are not discussed here for expositional ease.

Thus in the case of walking the simple model predicts 62% of the reported participation of respondents. Of the individual independent variables, age and sex of respondents are statistically significant as described above, with the chance of a type 1 error being set at 5%. The sex coefficient reveals that being female reduces the log odds of participation in walking. Finally, income has no statistically significant effect on participation.

In the case of swimming, all the coefficients are statistically significant and the model predicts over 80% of the reported participation of respondents. In particular the coefficients tell us that increases in income increase the chance of participation in contrast with increasing age. Finally, and in contrast with walking, the results show that it is more likely that females participate in swimming than males.

For keep fit/yoga activities, once again, all the regression coefficients are statistically significant. Of particular note is the sex variable, which implies that being female increases the chances of participation in keep fit/yoga activity. Standing in contrast is the case of soccer. Here, the results reveal that income has no statistically significant effect on participation In contrast, increases in age will reduce the log-odds of participating. Finally, the coefficient reveals that being female is strongly and negatively associated with the log-odds ratio of participation in soccer in contrast with keep fit/yoga and swimming.

Thus, in general, this modelling exercise reaffirms the findings implied in the descriptive analysis. In these specific cases, however, they reveal the importance that age, and particularly sex, has on participation. It follows that these factors are likely to have an impact on the demands in markets for sports and leisure activities and equipment more generally.

Some summary comments

The above analysis offers some discussion of the main theoretical reasons why variables measuring the tastes or constraints of consumers in the sports, leisure and tourism markets should be incorporated into an analysis of demand in these areas. Drawing on official data from the GHS, the relevance of these ideas has been demonstrated using descriptive and inferential analysis. In particular it has been shown that these variables offer some key understanding in the relative size of markets as well as potential market segments. Drawing on the idea of derived demand, moreover, it is clear that these findings have a direct relevance to those not interested in participation *per se* but also those supplying this market, such as sports equipment and clothing manufacturers. Figure 4.5 thus draws on Figure 4.2 to illustrate how official data might aid business decision-makers to understand their market. The figure summarises a two-stage process in which knowledge of the reasons for participation can be understood directly, but subsequently inform the analysis of derived markets.

---

7 The test is conducted as a chi-square test based on one degree of freedom. The test statistic is calculated as the square of the quotient based on dividing the estimated coefficient by the standard error of the estimated coefficient.

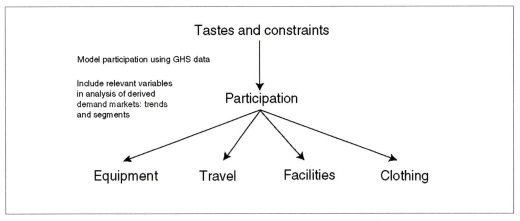

Figure 4.5   Applying the model showing the structure of demand for sports, leisure and tourism

Relationships with commercial data

Before closing it is worth highlighting some contrasts with commercially produced data on the sports, leisure and tourism markets. MINTEL, for example, regularly produces reports on a wide range of associated markets. One of the main problems with using such data is that the sample sizes tend to be much smaller and thus are, to a degree, less representative. In particular MINTEL analyses only those who participate in an activity whereas the GHS also covers those who do not participate in a particular activity. In this respect analysing the GHS data, as for example illustrated above, controls for sample-selection bias. Another problem is that the raw data are unavailable for statistical analysis unlike the official data.

On the other hand the MINTEL reports are updated frequently, which makes the analysis of trends more straightforward. Moreover, to an extent analysing the changes in variables may remove the biases noted above if they are of similar magnitudes in each survey. Often there is also a detailed analysis of particular components of the market in terms of age, sex, social class and region. In this respect the analysis can be cross-checked against official sources. This would be a useful exercise because MINTEL also provides some data on the relative frequency of participation differentiating between any, occasional and frequent participation, which adds a valuable dimension to the understanding of demand.

MINTEL also presents the analysis of how participation is affected by particular household characteristics such as the presence of children, older families with children having left home, and so on. Similar information is, of course, collected as part of the GHS in describing the characteristics of households but not presented in a pre-packaged form. In addition, data on educational background and health are also collected in the GHS to help to provide a more complete picture of participation. To analyse these factors the raw data need to be analysed. Consequently, in general there is a trade-off between the quality of information as provided by official sources and the need to spend effort analysing it.

Conclusion

This chapter has outlined alternative views of the broader structure of demands for sports, leisure and tourism, identifying participation as having a central place in this structure. To probe more deeply into this relationship it outlined how various theories of demand may be related and suggests a common structure of models. Conceptual and measurement issues associated with modelling participation were discussed and then illustrated using data from the GHS. The final section shows how official data can be combined with data provided by commercial organisations to provide further understanding of demand. Important caveats are attached to the use of commercially produced data.

5 Explaining tourism demand

Dr Ramesh Durbarry and Professor M Thea Sinclair Christel DeHaan Tourism and Travel Research Institute, University of Nottingham

Focus questions

- Why is knowledge of tourism demand important?
- How can economic theory help to explain tourism demand?
- How can statistical data be used to describe tourism demand?

- How can elasticities of demand be measured?
- How can elasticities of demand help policy-makers?
- What is an appropriate measure of the price of tourism?

Introduction

Statistical data can be used both to describe and to explain the demand for tourism. Explanations of tourism demand are useful because of the effects that tourist arrivals and expenditure have on destinations and because they can assist policy formulation. As discussed in Chapter 4, through the framework of derived demand, increases in tourist numbers result in greater demand for goods, services and infrastructure, while changes in expenditure by tourists have indirect and induced effects on income and employment across the economy. The balance of payments is also affected, as rising expenditure by foreign tourists provides increases in foreign currency availability, contributing to an improvement in the current account. Conversely, expenditure abroad by domestic residents constitutes an outflow that worsens the current account, contributing to possible pressure on the government to implement deflationary policies to avoid further deterioration. No less important are the effects that tourism demand has on income distribution and levels of welfare.

In the light of the effects that changes in tourism demand bring about, it is necessary to understand the reasons why such changes may occur. Hence, the focus of this chapter is on using data to go beyond descriptions of tourist arrivals and expenditure, to provide explanations of tourism demand. The discussion will be concerned with describing trends in tourism demand and with explaining how models of tourism demand can be used to estimate the sensitivity of demand to changes in the economic variables on which it depends. Key variables that will be considered are income (expenditure), relative prices and exchange rates, all of which can experience significant changes over time, and knowledge about the extent to which such changes affect tourism demand in the destinations under consideration is useful to both the private and public sectors.

The discussion in the chapter will proceed as follows. The following section will be concerned with showing the ways in which data can be used to describe and quantify the demand for tourism, using the case of the UK. This will provide a context for the following explanation of the models that can be used to estimate the extent to which demand changes in response to changes in key economic variables. Some results for the UK will be provided. Although tourism demand can also be affected by 'non-economic' variables, for example marketing campaigns to influence the destination image, they will not be considered here. The final section will provide some results and conclusions.

Using data to describe tourism demand

Domestic tourism demand

Tourism is increasing worldwide by around 4–5% per annum while domestic tourism tends to grow more slowly, at around 3% per annum (Turner and Reisinger, 2001). Although the scope to generate inflows of foreign currency has increased the significance of international tourism, domestic tourism has considerable potential to raise income and employment through the economic multiplier effect. In fact, domestic tourism accounts for more than 50% of total tourism in many countries, and more than 50% of tourism demand within some regions of the same country; for instance, in the UK it is around 50–65% of total demand (StarUK, 2002) and in Turkey, domestic tourism constitutes by far the largest share of tourism in the eastern provinces (Seckelmann, 2002).

However, little research has been undertaken on domestic tourism, mainly because of constraints on data availability. Data on domestic tourism can be obtained from tourist boards or national statistical offices (particularly from household budget surveys). In the UK, for example, data can be obtained through the English Tourism Council, the British Tourist Authority, Household Budget Surveys and the Office for National Statistics. Studies of domestic tourism have tended to adopt a descriptive approach and often limit their analysis to a particular region. This section of the chapter will focus on the data that can be used to describe domestic tourism demand, while the models that can be used to estimate demand will be discussed in the next section.

In 2000 the value of tourism in the UK was £75 billion. UK residents made 175.4 million trips within the UK spending more than £26 billion, compared with 25.2 million tourists who arrived from abroad and spent around £12.8 billion. The importance of domestic tourism relative to international tourism in the UK can be seen in Table 5.1, which shows that domestic and international tourist numbers and expenditure have been growing during recent years. The increase in the demand for domestic tourism is also clear from the Family Expenditure Survey, which shows that the real weekly expenditure on holidays by UK households has been increasing over the years (Figure 5.1).

International tourism demand

The number of tourist arrivals from abroad is a particularly obvious measure of international tourism demand. As increasing numbers of tourists generate additional demand for goods, services and infrastructure, it is useful to have some knowledge of the trends in demand. In the case of the UK, the numbers of tourist arrivals have grown considerably over time, as shown in Figure 5.2.

Table 5.1 Domestic and international tourism in the UK, 1995–2000

Year	Tourism trips (millions)		Tourism nights (millions)		Tourism spending (£ millions)	
	UK residents	Overseas residents	UK residents	Overseas residents	UK residents	Overseas residents
1995	121.0	23.5	449.8	220.3	12,775	11,763
1996	127.0	25.2	454.6	219.8	13,895	12,290
1997	133.6	25.5	473.6	222.5	15,075	12,244
1998	122.3	25.7	437.6	230.8	14,030	12,671
1999	146.1	25.4	495.3	211.7	16,255	12,498
2000[1]	175.4	25.2	576.4	203.8	26,132	12,805

Source: StarUK (2002)

1 Owing to changes in methodology, figures for UK residents in 2000 are not directly comparable with preceding years.

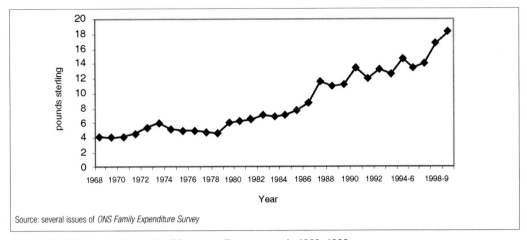

Source: several issues of *ONS Family Expenditure Survey*

Figure 5.1   UK households' real holiday expenditure per week, 1969–1999

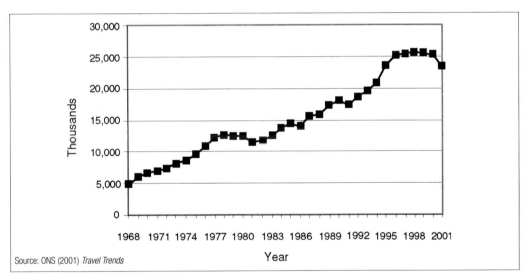

Source: ONS (2001) *Travel Trends*

Figure 5.2   Annual tourist arrivals in the UK from overseas, 1968–2001

Aggregate data, such as those depicted in Figure 5.2, are helpful in demonstrating the overall trends in tourist arrivals but do not reveal the differences in behaviour between nationalities. Therefore, data for arrivals by nationality were used to graph the trends relating to incoming tourists' country of origin, as shown in Figure 5.3. It can be seen that in contrast with the aggregate upward trend in total arrivals in the UK shown in Figure 5.2, arrivals from France, Belgium and Germany decreased between 1997 and 2000. Tourists come mainly from the USA, Japan, Australia and Europe; these tourists represent around 80% of total arrivals. Arrivals from the USA are particularly volatile.

The relative importance of arrivals from 11 major origin countries in 1998 to 2000 is shown in Figure 5.4. These countries account for around 70% of tourists visiting the UK annually. In 2000, the USA was the most important origin in terms of tourist numbers, followed by France, Germany, the Irish Republic, the Netherlands, Belgium, Italy, Spain, Australia, Switzerland and Japan.

Trends in the UK's share of international tourism receipts

The UK's earnings from overseas tourism have increased over time, although its share of

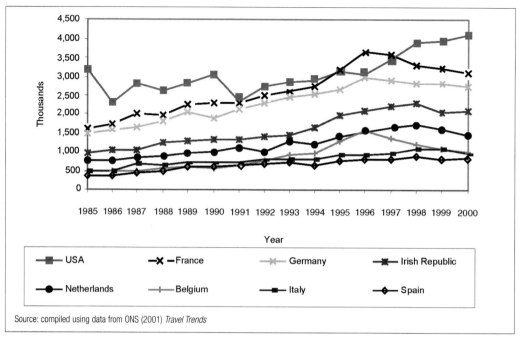

Figure 5.3   Annual tourist arrivals in the UK, 1985–2000

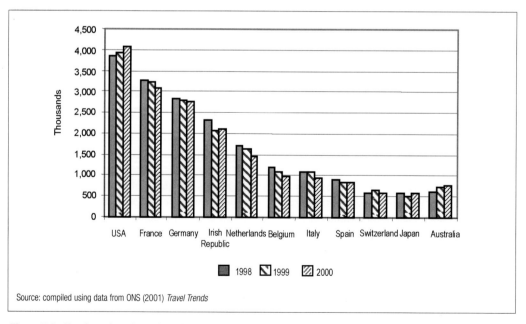

Figure 5.4   Number of tourist arrivals in the UK, 1998–2000

international tourism receipts has deteriorated, as shown in Figure 5.5. The decline in the UK's share began in 1980–1, following the increase in the rate of value added tax applicable to tourism and other services from 8% to 15% (subsequently increased to 17.5% in 1991; HM Customs and Excise annual reports). Since then, the UK's share of international tourism receipts has declined gradually to around 4.5% in the mid 1990s. In 2000, with the exception of the USA, main tourist destinations such as France, Spain, Italy and the UK witnessed a fall in their tourism receipts. There is evidence to suggest that the UK is losing its share of the world market, both in terms of arrivals and receipts; China, in particular, is emerging as an important comparatively new destination (see Table 5.2). It is clear from Table 5.2 that the market shares of the USA, France, Italy and Spain considerably exceed that of the UK, in terms of tourist arrivals and international tourism receipts.

Current and real tourism earnings in the UK

The growth in tourism receipts for the period 1978–2000 in current and constant (real) terms is shown in Figure 5.6. The real tourism earnings figures were derived by deflating receipts from tourism expenditure by the tourism price index as discussed below. In simple terms an index number measures the percentage change in a variable over time relative to a base year. A price index thus measures the change in prices over time. Dividing tourism receipts by the price index thus accounts for inflation. The base year is 1995.[1]

The importance of this is that, as Figure 5.6 demonstrates, the growth over time in real tourism receipts has been fairly low, in contrast with the view that would emerge from inspection of the growth of receipts in current terms. Moreover, there was a decline in the real value of receipts at the end of the 1990s. Although tourism receipts from the USA continued to increase, receipts from other origins were either stagnating or falling in the late 1990s, as shown in Figure 5.7.

---

1 To illustrate how to derive an index number, consider the case if the number of tourism visitors was 2,000,000 in 1985 and 2,250,000 in 1992. If 1985 is considered as the base year, the index numbers would be (2,000,000/2,000,000) × 100 = 100 for 1985 and (2,250,000/2,000,000) × 100 = 112.5 for 1992. This would imply that the numbers of visitors rose by 12.5% over the period 1985 to 1992.

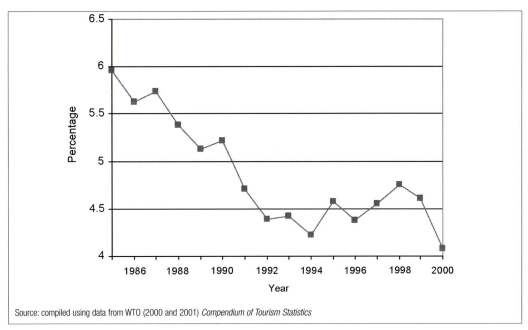

Source: compiled using data from WTO (2000 and 2001) *Compendium of Tourism Statistics*

Figure 5.5 UK's share of international tourism receipts, 1985–2000

Table 5.2   Market shares of main destinations, 1999 and 2000

Country	International tourist arrivals (millions)		Market share (%)	International tourism receipts (US$ billions)		Market share (%)
	1999	2000	2000	1999	2000	2000
France	73.0	75.5	10.8	31.5	29.9	6.3
USA	48.5	50.9	7.3	74.9	85.2	17.9
Spain	46.8	48.2	6.9	32.4	31.0	6.5
Italy	36.5	41.2	5.9	28.4	27.4	5.8
China	27.0	31.2	4.5	14.1	16.2	3.4
UK	25.4	25.2	3.6	20.2	19.5	4.1
Germany	17.1	19.0	2.7	16.7	17.8	3.7
World	650.4	698.8	100.0	455.4	475.8	100.0

Source: WTO (2001) *Compendium of Tourism Statistics*

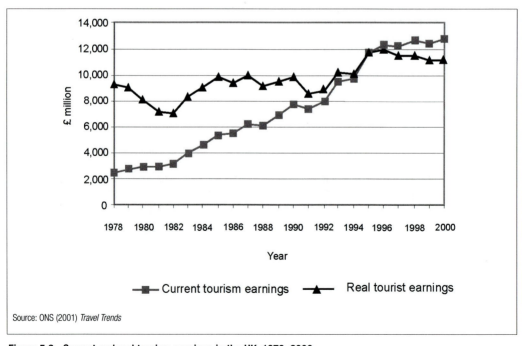

Source: ONS (2001) *Travel Trends*

Figure 5.6   Current and real tourism earnings in the UK, 1978–2000

In recent years tourism receipts have decreased in real terms for most countries, excluding the USA. The increase in tourism receipts from the USA was mainly the result of considerable increases in the number of tourist arrivals; for instance, for the period 1997–8 tourist arrivals increased by 13%. For some other countries, such as France, Germany, Belgium, Japan and Australia, tourist arrivals decreased during the same period, as was shown in Figure 5.3. Overall, tourist arrivals increased slightly, by around 1% between 1997 and 1998, while real tourism earnings increased by only 0.3%.

It is clear that tourist arrivals and tourism receipts have changed differently over time and that increases in arrivals have not been accompanied by proportionate increases in receipts. As discussed in Chapter 7, it is also important to examine changes in the amounts that tourists spend per visit in real terms. Real average tourism earnings per visit by country of origin are shown in Figure 5.8.

The trends reveal that there is cause for concern regarding real expenditure per visit in the UK by overseas residents. In fact, for most of the countries, real average spending per visit has declined over recent years. For example, although total real tourist earnings and tourist arrivals from the USA have been rising in recent years, real average expenditure per visit has fallen.

The Tourism Price Index and effective exchange rates

Most studies use the consumer price index as an indicator of the cost of tourism in a particular country. This is an index that measures the price of a 'basket' of consumer items. An important caveat when using the consumer price index to reflect the cost of tourism is that the basket of goods and services included are those purchased by UK residents, rather than those purchased by tourists. A list of items that tourists purchase is available from the International Passenger Survey, as exemplified in Table 5.3. A price index based on these items would be more appropriate for measuring the cost of tourism than the consumer price index. In the UK, the Office for National Statistics computes retail

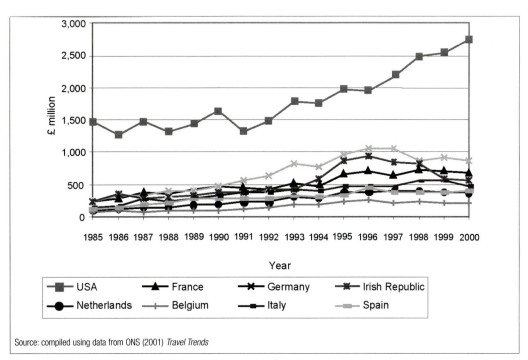

Source: compiled using data from ONS (2001) *Travel Trends*

Figure 5.7   Tourism receipts by main country of origin in the UK, 1985–2000

price indices for goods and services that tourists consume. Figure 5.9 shows the consumer and tourism price indices using 1990 as the base year. Both indices show a rising trend over the years, but it is obvious that these indices are not synonymous. In fact, for the UK it can be observed that prices of goods and services consumed by tourists have risen more than the prices of all goods and services. For instance, during the period 1990–2000, tourism prices increased by 3.5% per annum, on average,

while the consumer price index increased by only 2.7%. Hence, use of the consumer price index would understate the cost of tourism. Furthermore, the tourism price index would have been higher if changes in air passenger duty had been included.

Exchange rates are sometimes used to represent tourists' cost of living. Exchange rates affect tourists' decisions in choosing particular destinations and their expenditure on arrival. In many studies, the

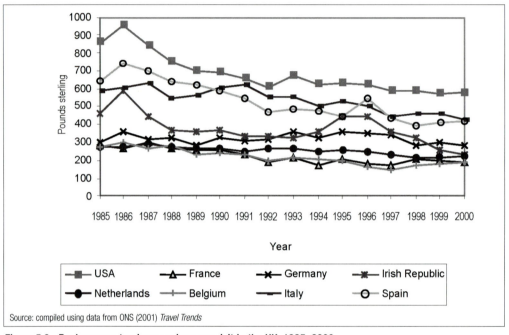

Source: compiled using data from ONS (2001) *Travel Trends*

Figure 5.8   Real average tourism earnings per visit in the UK, 1985–2000

Table 5.3   Percentage of overseas visitors' spending by year and spending category, 1979, 1986, 1992 and 1997

Spending category	1979	1986	1992	1997
Accommodation	27.5	32.3	36.1	33.3
Eating out and alcohol	14.7	22.5	21.9	20.6
Travel within UK	11.5	8.6	7.8	9.2
Clothes	19.9	14.1	12.6	12.8
Other shopping	15.9	13.0	11.9	13.2
Other expenditure	10.5	9.5	9.5	10.9
Total	100	100	100	100

Source: ONS (1999) *Travel Trends*

exchange rate has been used as a separate variable for representing the price of tourism in that appreciation or depreciation of the exchange rate directly affects tourism costs. Exchange-rate appreciation is likely to reduce tourism expenditure in a destination. Perhaps a better indicator would be exchange rates adjusted by price changes to account for inflation. In this respect, the real effective exchange rate index would be a better indicator than the level of the exchange rate. An increase (decrease) in the real effective exchange rate index would indicate appreciation (depreciation), implying an increased (decreased) cost of tourism. Figure 5.10 depicts the percentage change in the real effective exchange rate of the UK and percentage change in average tourism expenditure. From the figure, it seems that appreciation (depreciation) of the real exchange rate induces average tourism spending to fall (increase).

The effect of exchange rate appreciation or depreciation on total tourism earnings is more obvious from Figure 5.11. It can be observed that changes in the real effective exchange rate and changes in total tourism earnings are negatively associated.

The discussions of UK tourism in this section have shown that although the sector has experienced significant growth in arrivals from overseas, declines in arrivals from some countries occurred in the latter part of the 1990s. The growth of real tourism receipts from abroad has been fairly low and real tourism receipts per capita per tourist visit have decreased for many of the UK's major origin countries. This may be related to the increasing real price of tourism in the UK. The tourism price index for the UK has risen faster than the consumer price index and the effective exchange rate for sterling increased considerably during the 1990s, making the UK yet more expensive for tourists from abroad.

Overall, it is clear that the tourism industry in the UK is facing problems, particularly in the form of a falling share of world tourism receipts, decreasing price competitiveness and falls in the value of receipts per tourist visit from key origin countries. This is the context against which the discussion of

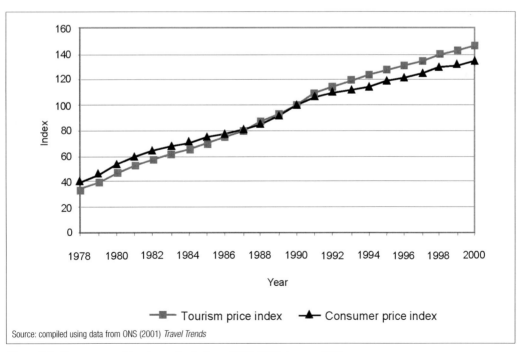

Source: compiled using data from ONS (2001) *Travel Trends*

Figure 5.9   Consumer and tourism price indices, 1979–2001, base = 1990

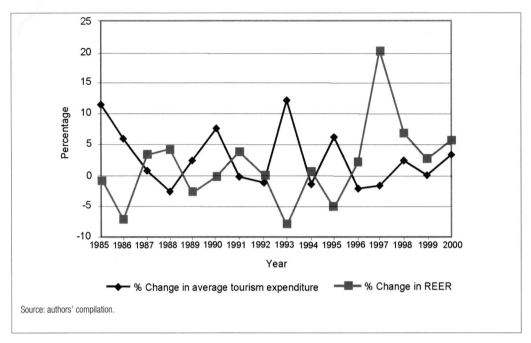

Figure 5.10   Percentage change in the real effective exchange rate and in tourism earnings, 1970–2000 (1985 = 100)

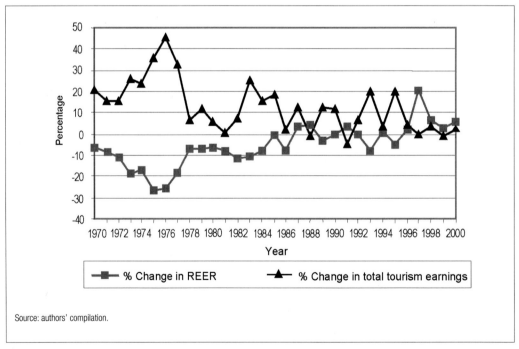

Figure 5.11   Percentage change in the real effective exchange rate and in tourism earnings, 1970–2000 (1985=100)

the models that can be used to estimate the sensitivity of tourism demand to changes in its major economic determinants, such as changes in prices, must be considered.

Explaining tourism demand

The use of models

Models serve the purpose of simplifying a complex real world situation so as to provide an explanation of the phenomenon under consideration. For example, in the case of tourism demand, models can be used to examine whether tourism demand is affected by variables on which it is hypothesised to depend. Models can also quantify the extent to which demand changes in response to a change in each of the variables and provide forecasts of the likely changes in future demand. In this section we will concentrate on the models that examine the sensitivity of tourism demand to changes in key economic variables to extend the discussion of Chapter 4, as models for tourism demand forecasting are discussed, for example, in Chapter 6.

As Chapter 4 explains, economic theory argues that the key variables on which demand depends are income and prices. Consumers obtain income from paid work and/or other sources such as dividends or benefits, which provides them with a budget for expenditure on goods and services. In the case of a normal product, higher income will result in higher demand, with the opposite occurring for the case of an inferior product. Conversely, a rise in the price of the product generally brings about in a fall in demand. A fall in demand also occurs if there is a fall in the price of a product that is a substitute of the product under consideration, such as a holiday in a competing destination. Demand for the product rises if there is a fall in the price of a complement, such as the price of admission to a major attraction in the area. Hence, the demand for tourism depends on income, on the price of the tourism product (as discussed in the earlier section on tourism price indices) and on its price relative to the prices of substitutes and/or complements (Sinclair and Stabler, 1997). Demand also depends on relative exchange rates in the case of tourism in countries with different currencies.

Models of tourism demand are able to explain whether these variables are significant determinants of demand in specific cases as discussed in Chapter 4. The sensitivity of demand to a change in each of the variables can be quantified using the results from the model. A useful quantitative measure in the current context is the ratio of the percentage change in demand in response to 1% change in the variable under consideration. This is known as the elasticity value relating to a small change in the variable. Elasticities are unit-free measures of sensitivity so they allow the researcher to make an easy comparison of the strength of impact of variables on demand. The sign of the elasticity value informs the researcher about the direction in which the variables move. Thus one would usually expect the value of an own price elasticity to be negative and the value of an income elasticity to be positive. This would indicate that a rise in the own price of the good or service would decrease demand for it and a rise in income would increase demand (and vice-versa for a fall in the value of the variables). An elastic response is indicated for values greater than '1' in absolute terms – regardless of sign. This suggests that a given percentage change in a variable will lead to a greater percentage change in demand. Elasticity values of less than '1' in absolute terms indicate inelastic responses, as given percentage changes in a variable lead to smaller percentage changes in demand.

Knowledge of the elasticity values is useful for policy formulation. For example, information about the income elasticity values for tourists from different origins can help to identify the tourist origin countries towards which marketing efforts can be directed, and for which an increase in income will result in high increases in demand. Knowledge of the price elasticity values is useful for the formulation of pricing policy vis-à-vis competitors. It is also relevant to policies relating to changes in subsidies or taxation (noted in ONS *Inland Revenue Statistics* and the Customs and Excise *Annual Report of the Commissioners of Customs and Excise*), when combined with information about the degree to which changes are passed on in the form of changes in the prices that are charged to tourists.

Thus, following the discussion of Chapter 4, in the case of tourism demand modelling it might be hypothesised that tourism demand, D, depends on a number of key variables: $D = f(x_1, x_2, ... x_n)$. This relationship could then be investigated using multiple regression analysis to quantify the responsiveness of demand to a change in each of the variables. Two considerations are particularly important in the modelling process. The first is to ensure that the hypothesis is formulated using relevant theory as, without such a basis, any findings that indicate a significant relationship between the dependent variable and its possible determinants may be spurious. The second is to use appropriate econometric techniques to investigate the possible relationship and to test the results that are obtained. The relevance of these considerations to tourism demand modelling will now be considered.

Tourism demand modelling has progressed from early studies that tended to specify the relationship between tourism demand and its possible determinants in a fairly *ad hoc* way to more recent studies that use economic theory as the basis for specifying tourism demand equations, which are then estimated using rigorous econometric techniques. Thus, early studies are characterised by a variety of different specifications of tourism demand equations; for example, some included either prices or exchange rates as possible determinants of demand, some included both, while others included exchange rates weighted by prices, without explaining the rationale for the choice of the variables. Subsequent research, notably by Syriopoulos (1995), used the 'general to specific' methodology to specify a general set of possible variables determining demand, which is then reduced to a smaller set of significant determinants by means of econometric tests.

More recent studies have used an explicit theoretical basis, founded on consumer demand theory, to underpin the specification of tourism demand equations (for example, Syriopoulos and Sinclair, 1993; Papatheodorou, 1999; De Mello *et al.*, 2002). Econometric methods for estimating a non-spurious long-term relationship between tourism demand and its possible determinants have also been used to take account of the adjustment of tourism demand to its determinants (Song *et al.*, 2000; De Mello, 2001; Durbarry, 2002; Pulina, 2002). As discussed

in Chapter 6, time-series data may be non-stationary. In these cases it is possible to produce a spurious regression unless the data are made stationary first.

An exception is cointegration analysis, which can identify a long-term relationship. The details of this approach are beyond the scope of this book. The more recent studies also use a range of other econometric tests to check for possible statistical problems such as mis-specification bias and to examine the significance of the results. The type of modelling that is undertaken and the results that it can provide will now be illustrated using examples of inbound and outbound tourism for the UK.

Modelling consumer decision-making

Different models can be formulated to explain different phenomena. Economic models of consumer decision-making can help to explain the ways in which consumers allocate their expenditure budgets between different goods and services. A well known model within the field of consumer decision-making is the Almost Ideal Demand System (AIDS) model developed by Deaton and Muellbauer (1980a; 1980b). The model has the advantage of an explicit basis in economic theory, is easy to estimate and provides information that is useful for policy-making. It also has a history of application in the area of tourism demand dating back to White (1982) and O'Hagan and Harrison (1984) and will be discussed within this and the following section.

The AIDS model posits that consumers allocate their expenditure between goods and services by means of a stage budgeting process. In the first stage, expenditure is allocated between major categories of products, such as food, accommodation and tourism. The next stage involves the allocation of expenditure between products in each of the categories, for instance, tourism in different destinations of the world, such as the country of residence, other countries within Europe or other regions (North America, Central and South America, Africa, Asia, Australia and New Zealand). The subsequent stage may involve the allocation of expenditure between individual countries within each of the regions and a further stage may involve expenditure allocation between different types of tourism within individual countries. The modelling often focuses on explaining consumers' allocation of expenditure within one of the stages of the process, involving the assumption that the decisions taken within one stage of the budgeting process are independent of decisions taken in another. In the case of past studies of tourism demand, models have typically focused on the allocation of expenditure between individual countries within a set of country destinations.

The model involves a number of assumptions about consumer behaviour. The main assumption is that consumers behave rationally. Hence, if prices rise, demand is assumed to decrease. Consistency of behaviour is assumed, so that if destination A is preferred to destination B, and B is preferred to C, then A is also preferred to C. Further assumptions are that proportionate changes in prices and expenditure have no effect on the quantities purchased, and that the shares of the total budget that are spent on the products (countries) in the set under consideration sum to unity. Detailed derivation of the model is provided in previous studies (see, for example, Syriopoulos and Sinclair, 1993; De Mello *et al.*, 2002; Durbarry, 2002), giving rise to the general equation below to be estimated:

$$w_i = \alpha_i + \sum_j \gamma_{ij} \ln p_j + \beta_i \ln \left(\frac{x}{P} \right)$$

where the dependent variable w_i represents destination i's share of the origin's tourism budget allocated to the set of n destinations. This share's variability is explained by the price of tourism, p, in destination i and in alternative destinations j and by the per capita expenditure, x, allocated to the group of n destinations, deflated by price index P. The effective price variable takes account of both prices and exchange rates. The share of the consumer's budget that is allocated to different countries within the set depends on the overall budget and on relative prices, as argued by economic theory. The values of the coefficients γ_{ij} and β_i indicate the extent to which the expenditure share changes in response to changes in the log (ln) values of relative prices and real expenditure per capita.

Information about the sensitivity of tourism demand to changes in expenditure and relative effective prices for a range of tourist origins and destinations can be obtained by estimating a full set of equations,

relating to all the origin and destination countries under consideration, using multiple regression analysis. This provides quantitative measures (coefficient values) showing the extent to which the budget share for each destination (the measure of tourism demand) changes in response to changes in the total expenditure budget and in the relative prices of the different origins and destinations. The calculation of elasticity values constitutes the usual way of comparing the sensitivity of demand to variations in its determining variables. The expenditure elasticities are measures of the change in demand in response to a change in the expenditure budget and can be calculated using the formula $\varepsilon_i = (\beta_i / w_i) + 1$. The price elasticities measure the change in demand in response to a change in the price of the origin relative to the destination (the own price elasticity) or in the price of the origin relative to an alternative destination (the substitute price elasticity). They can be calculated using the formula

$$\varepsilon_{ii} = (\gamma_{ii} / w_i) - \beta_i - 1$$

for the own price elasticities and

$$\varepsilon_{ij} = (\gamma_{ij} / w_i) - \beta_i (w_j / w_i)$$

for the cross price elasticities.

Price and expenditure sensitivities of UK tourism demand

The types of information about tourism demand that can be obtained by estimating the AIDS model are illustrated by two case studies. The first relates to tourist expenditure in the UK, Italy and Spain by French tourists, who constitute the second largest market for the UK after the USA. The second is concerned with UK tourist expenditure in France, Portugal and Spain, which receive a considerable share of UK expenditure abroad. The time period that was considered for the first case, relating to French tourists' expenditure in the UK, was 1968–99 and the AIDS model was estimated using long-run structural modelling methods (Durbarry, 2002; Pesaran and Shin, 1999). The values of the elasticities, giving the sensitivities of tourism demand to changes in expenditure and relative effective prices, are shown in Table 5.4.

Table 5.4 Uncompensated own price and cross price, and expenditure elasticities for UK, Spain and Italy

Destinations	Price elasticities			Expenditure elasticities
	UK	Spain	Italy	
UK	−1.721	0.700	−0.081[†]	1.103
Spain	0.243	−1.823	0.525	1.088
Italy	0.025[†]	0.994	−1.902	0.791

Source: Durbarry (2002)

† indicates not significant at 5% level

The elasticity values were calculated using budget shares in the base year; use of the latest year did not significantly change the values.

The values of the own price elasticities (shown in italic along the diagonal in the table) indicate that, for each of the destinations, an increase in its own prices relative to prices in France results in a large and significant decrease in demand. For example, for the case of the UK, a 1% increase in UK prices relative to prices in France results in a decrease in demand of 1.7%. The own price elasticity values for Spain and Italy indicate slightly larger falls in demand, of 1.8% and 1.9% respectively, in response to rises in prices. The cross price elasticity values, shown by the remaining values in the table, indicate the sensitivity of demand in one destination in response to a change in prices in another destination, which is a potential competitor. For example, French demand for the UK increases by 0.7% in response to a 1% increase in prices in Spain, whereas French demand for Spain increases by only 0.2% in response to a 1% increase in prices in the UK. The elasticity values for Italy are not significant.

The value of the expenditure elasticity for the UK indicates that a 1% increase in the total expenditure budget leads to a 1.1% increase in demand. The expenditure elasticity value for Spain is virtually the same as that for the UK, while the value for Italy is lower. Hence, although the UK appears to benefit from an increase in the total expenditure budget for the French, the increase is not much greater than unity.

The second study provides information about the sensitivity of the UK's demand for tourism in neighbouring Mediterranean countries to changes in effective prices and expenditure (De Mello et al., 2002). The time period considered was 1969–97 and the seemingly unrelated regressions (SUR) approach was used to estimate the model. The elasticity values are calculated for the sub-period 1980–97, following the 'shocks' to tourism demand caused by major political changes in Spain and Portugal, and are given in Table 5.5.

The own price elasticity values (shown in italic along the diagonal) indicate that the UK's tourism demand for each of the destinations is highly

Table 5.5 Uncompensated own price and cross price, and expenditure elasticities for France, Spain and Portugal

Destinations	Price elasticities			Expenditure elasticities
	France	Spain	Portugal	
France	−1.90	1.08	0.02[†]	0.81
Spain	0.66	−1.93	0.12	1.15
Portugal	0.02[†]	0.83	−1.90	0.95

Source: De Mello et al. (2002)

† indicates not significant at 5% level

sensitive to an increase in the effective price of the destination relative to UK prices. In each case, an increase of 1% in the effective price of the destination results in a fall in UK demand approaching 2%. The cross price elasticity values are low and are insignificant in the case of tourism demand for France with respect to an increase in Portuguese prices and demand for Portugal with respect to an increase in French prices. This indicates that UK tourists' demand for a specific destination does not appear to be very sensitive to changes in the prices of that destination relative to its competitors.

Conclusions

Domestic tourism demand for the UK is increasing in terms of numbers of tourist arrivals and expenditure. International tourism demand is increasing in terms of the numbers of arrivals; however, real tourism receipts have tended to stabilise in recent years and receipts from some major origin countries and receipts per tourist arrival have declined. At the same time, expenditure abroad by UK tourists is rising, in real terms. Hence, examination of the data for tourist arrivals and receipts has demonstrated that the UK is facing challenges in terms of the net contribution of tourism to income and employment generation and the balance of payments.

Models that help to explain the changes in tourism demand, as well as the extent of the changes that occur, provide useful information for policy-makers. The case studies of the UK have shown that the demand for tourism in the UK from one of its major markets, France, is highly sensitive to changes in relative effective prices. Thus if the UK loses price competitiveness, for example because of an appreciation in the exchange rate for sterling, it will experience a considerable fall in demand for tourism from the French market. UK residents who travel abroad are also very sensitive to changes in the prices of neighbouring Mediterranean destinations relative to the UK, so that relative price competitiveness is also important for outbound tourism from the UK.

Exchange rates and relative rates of inflation both contribute to changes in real effective prices, so that

government policies that affect either exchange rates or inflation can cause a change in net tourism demand. Although membership of a common currency regime, such as the Euro, would eliminate one source of changing demand, changes in relative rates of inflation would still cause net changes in receipts between origin and destination countries. Therefore there is a case for policy-makers to take account of the effects on tourism when formulating macro-economic policies that affect exchange rates and/or inflation, particularly in countries in which tourism plays a large role in the economy. Government policies concerning taxes that fall on goods and services consumed by tourists also affect net tourism demand to the extent that the taxes are passed on to the tourist consumers, so there is also a case for taking account of the implications for tourism demand of changes in taxation.

The cross price elasticity values for tourism demand tend to be low relative to the own price elasticities, implying that UK tourists take little account of the relative competitiveness between destinations but are much more aware of the competitiveness between their own country and specific destinations under consideration. Thus it is possible that the information that tourists use in their decision-making is limited to that which is most easily available and intelligible, which has implications for the marketing of destinations to potential tourists.

The expenditure elasticity values did not depart greatly from unity, indicating that the UK will not experience major gains from an increase in the total expenditure budget of French tourists. Similarly, the expenditure shares of the Mediterranean countries to which UK tourists travel will not experience major changes as the result of a change in the expenditure budget of the UK. Explanation of the possible reasons for these findings requires more information, at the micro-economic level, concerning differences between socio-economic groups, the content and effectiveness of marketing campaigns and supply-side factors including the quality of tourism provision.

Overall, it is clear that data analysis can help to identify key trends in tourism demand and the issues and problems that may exist. Models of tourism demand can provide explanations of past and current changes in demand and provide information that is relevant to policy formulation. Particular models are directed towards explaining particular phenomena. The AIDS model is helpful in explaining the tourist decision-making process and in quantifying the effects on demand of changes in relative prices and the tourist expenditure budget. Different models are likely to be appropriate for explaining other issues, such as the role of distance and transportation in tourism demand, using the gravity model (Durbarry, 2000) or the travel cost model (Brown Jr and Henry, 1989). The values of different characteristics of the tourism product could be explained by using models such as the hedonic pricing model (Sinclair et al., 1990; Clewer et al., 1992; Aguiló et al., 2001) or the contingent valuation model (Lockwood et al., 1993; Lindberg and Johnson, 1997). Hence, the choice of model and the related data should be tailored to the issue or question under investigation.

6 Forecasting tourism demand

Alistair Dawson Division of Economics, Staffordshire University

Focus questions

- Why forecast demand?
- Are forecasts objective or subjective?
- What are desirable properties of forecasts?

- Should forecasts be combined?
- How are forecasts evaluated?

Introduction

This chapter addresses the reasons why people forecast demand and how they should proceed to do so; it also considers the choice of forecasting methods available. It should be noted that the emphasis is on 'time series' forecasting methods, that is methods that forecast demand from past observations on demand only; this is primarily for ease of exposition. Forecasting can also proceed econometrically, using the models discussed in Chapters 4 and 5. The evaluation of the forecasts can proceed as discussed in this chapter. However, there are also complications.[1]

The next section briefly explains why forecasting is important, reviews the complexity of markets in tourism and considers how this affects forecasting. In particular it considers how tourist activity is currently measured and looks at other, perhaps preferable, alternatives. Some simple methods of time series forecasting are then discussed and applied to ONS data. A key message of the chapter is that predicting economic events accurately and making effective use of such predictions is very difficult.

Why forecast demand?

Virtually every conscious decision we make is related to a forecast and the time horizons over which we forecast and the consequences of forecasts can vary. Thus, we can forecast in the very short run whether or not a coach excursion will run on time, or we could try to forecast whether or not it would be profitable to open a new hotel in a given resort. The complexity of these forecasts differs, as do the commercial consequences of getting forecasts radically wrong.

This suggests that we need to consider how best to make forecasts in particular situations and how to evaluate the alternatives. One can begin with a consideration of some desirable properties of forecasts in general.

Some desirable properties of forecasts

In general one can distinguish between subjective forecasts based on opinion only and objective methods that apply some replicable formula. Subjective forecasting is widely applied – often there is no alternative – in deriving firm-specific or brand-specific forecasts from general background data. However, even if the firm gets it right today it cannot guarantee doing so tomorrow. This is because

---

1 In particular the values of the explanatory variables in the regression model also have to be forecasted, known as 'conditional' forecasting. The procedure thus adds statistical complications. There is also no guarantee that an explanatory model forecasts better than the simple methods discussed here. Consequently, in practice there is sometimes a trade-off between models that explain well and models that predict well. Intuitively, the reason is quite simple. In a time series model past demand is likely to be very closely related to future demand. In contrast, the inevitable errors involved in explaining demand first and then forecasting demand become compounded.

it can never learn either why it got some forecasts right or why others were badly wrong – the method draws on tacit knowledge only. Such a subjective 'skill', moreover, cannot readily be transferred between persons. This suggests that objective methods of forecasting are preferable to subjective ones.

The main reasons for this are that one would prefer a forecast that is based on an unbiased random variable with a constant variance. The desirable property 'unbiasedness' means that 'on average' the forecast is correct – the expected value (mean) of the forecast is the actual future value of the variable being forecast. A biased forecast tends to over-predict or under-predict, in other words its expected value is not equal to the true value. 'Constant variance' means the forecasts (if unbiased) are distributed about the (unknown) true value with a constant degree of 'spread' – the forecasting system does not tend to become more or less accurate the longer we use it. To avoid misunderstanding of the term 'constant variance', note that when a forecast is published its creator must specify not only what is being forecast but also the date when the forecast was made and that to which it applies. This is because the degree of spread will depend on the period of time projected forward. Consequently, it is logical to argue that objective methods can be assessed by such criteria whereas subjective methods cannot.

Apart from the bias and efficiency properties outlined above, however, forecasts should preferably be available in time for the user to take advantage of them. Inevitably there is a trade-off between relatively inaccurate forecasts that permit one to take avoiding action and very accurate ones that come too late. From the user's viewpoint they ought also to be as simple as possible to apply and as inexpensive as possible for a given standard of accuracy and timeliness. Considering the amount of data that must be gathered and processed and the skilled labour involved, running a forecasting function is expensive and small- to medium-sized firms might do better to buy forecasts from professional bodies noting that competing firms might do likewise. Last but not least, forecasts that can actually track turning points, for example the

onset of a business recession, are sometimes more valuable than ones that are good in an efficiency or bias sense. Moreover, a point that should not be overlooked, and which is discussed further below, is that making effective use of forecasts is difficult because it involves the application of a degree of subjective judgement even if the basic formula is clearly stated.

Interdependent markets and forecasting

Before discussing the operational aspects of objective methods of forecasting one should pay some attention to the subject matter. Demand is highly complex in tourism, and indeed sports and leisure generally, as discussed in Chapters 4 and 5. Thus, in tourism one might begin with a simple concept such as the demand to visit a given country, region or resort. Related to this, however, are demands for transport to and from various points of origin, for accommodation at the resort and for access to transport and refreshments once there. To quantify or to predict 'demand' it is vital to determine which demand is the relevant one and how it relates to the others.

To begin with, assume that from the International Passenger Survey the total number of UK holiday visits to New York may be forecast for 2002. Hoteliers in particular would like also to know about average intended duration. This dimension is recognised by the International Passenger Survey, some of whose data are presented in the annual publication *Travel Trends*. Table 5.1 gives estimates of the annual visits to the UK by UK and overseas residents and of nights spent in the UK from 1995 to 2000. Duration is an essential dimension of tourist activity. Visitors who stay for six consecutive nights need only half the air miles but the same amount of bed space as those making two three-day trips. Since short and long breaks tend to be spent in different activities there are implications for other suppliers. Average duration figures, however, do not allow for seasonality. Other things being equal, the stronger the seasonal pattern the greater the number of beds needed to cope with peak demand.

The data also do not specify the split between single and double rooms or between family hotels and luxury hotels. They are based solely on mean duration and numbers expected to participate irrespective of age, sex, marital status, family composition, income and tastes. Finally, while UK tour operators may find data about UK residents' plans to visit New York very useful, New York hoteliers and theatre owners are interested primarily in the much greater total tourist flow into the city.

Furthermore, the forecaster who regards the demands for accommodation and flights as derived from demand for the ultimate activity – tourism itself – might infer that if tourist activity could be accurately forecast it would be relatively simple to derive good forecasts of input demands. While this argument is attractive one must not forget that the latter are not simply driven by tourist activity. Many people use air transport, restaurants and hotel accommodation while actively engaged on business, visiting families, and for other reasons not related to tourism. This also applies to sales of durable items such as new hotels and aeroplanes. Durable assets are purchased to make profits for their owners. The decision whether to purchase a new hotel depends on an estimate of the cash flow it is likely to generate over its expected life and on the returns available on alternative assets.

This suggests that investment in new tourist facilities is not likely to follow the number of visits closely. A 10% forecast permanent increase in visit levels to New York might (unless there is empty capacity) temporarily boost construction by more than 10%. Once capacity has reached the desired level, building activity will fall back to the replacement level. A 10% forecast permanent reduction in tourist activity may cause construction to cease altogether. The conclusion to be drawn from this is not that forecasts of overall tourist flows or tourist expenditure should be ignored by the industry but that users of even the best available overall forecasts must think very carefully about how the particular demand relevant to their business may alter, given the general background. Making effective use of forecasts is at least as important as making the forecasts themselves.

Some simple objective forecasting methods

To illustrate how to produce forecasts, this section lays out a set of common definitions to be used in all examples and a discussion of simple criteria that can be employed to evaluate forecasts. The next section applies a selection of simple objective forecasting methods to overseas residents' visits to the UK. As well as simple methods, insights into more sophisticated approaches are offered. Box 6.1 lists common forecasting definitions.

Box 6.1

Forecasting definitions

$A(t)$	The actual value of a variable at time t
$(t)F(t + 1)$	The one-step-ahead forecast F of variable of interest A at period $t + 1$ (made at period t)
$(t)F(t + 2)$	The corresponding two-step-ahead forecast made at period t
$F(t + 1)$	Simplified notation for one-step-ahead forecast
$e(t + 1) \equiv F(t + 1) - A(t + 1)$	The forecast error for one-step-ahead forecast
$(t)e(t + 2) \equiv (t)F(t + 2) - A(t + 2)$	The forecast error for two-step-ahead forecast

Of particular relevance is the difference between the forecast and the actual value, which is the forecast error. On this value hang many definitions of forecasting accuracy. Two important ones are the root mean square forecasting error (RMSFE) and mean absolute forecast error (MAFE). The formulae for these are shown in Box 6.2 on the basis that 'N' periods of data are analysed.

Box 6.2
Some simple evaluation criteria

The RMSFE	$\sqrt{(\Sigma(F - A)^2/N)}$
The MAFE	$(\Sigma|F - A|)/N$

To calculate RMSFE:

- Calculate all the errors made in forecasting variable A for (say) N periods.
- Square each error.
- Sum the squares.
- Obtain the mean square forecast error, an indicator of the 'spread' between forecast and actual values, by dividing the above sum by the number of forecasts, N.
- Compute the square root of the above expression to give the RMSFE. It indicates the magnitude (absolute value) of the average forecasting error; obviously the user would like this to be as small as possible.

The RMSFE is widely applied in evaluation and the smallest RMSFE is preferred if this is possible.

The reason for analysing the sum of squares is that first, it makes all the negative errors positive – if you summed all the errors the negative ones would offset positive ones, resulting in a very low average error. This explains why one squares *before* summing. You cannot tell whether any given average error results from having small (or very large) forecasting errors that just about cancel each other. By implication this means that the simple mean forecast error is useless in evaluation. Second, the RMSFE by squaring forecast errors punishes large errors in greater proportion than small ones. This may be an important consideration. If one under-predicts the profitability of a hotel development by 1% it is

unlikely that one would withdraw from the investment. If on the other hand one under-predicts by 5% one might do so and thereby lose a valuable opportunity.

In the case of the MAFE, the absolute error is just the positive value. So, again, negative errors are not allowed to offset positive ones, although this time small and big errors are punished in proportion. (The vertical brackets around the error $|F - A|$ mean that it is the absolute error, not the actual – positive or negative – that is being summed.) It should be noted in passing that the RMSFE and MAFE criteria may also be applied in percentage terms.

There are many other criteria related to RMSFE and to MAFE that attempt to summarise in a single number the ability of forecasters to hit the target. However, there are radically different ways of evaluating forecasts. For example, sometimes the user is interested not so much in getting 'close to' the target as in predicting whether the next movement will be up or down. Predicting the direction of exchange rate changes is very important to a firm that deals in several currencies. As forecasts do not usually perform well on all criteria, picking between them is not a simple matter. In general all that one can say is that there is no single 'ordering' of techniques suitable for all occasions.

Before showing how to produce and evaluate forecasts with reference to official data we need to distinguish between genuine *forecasting* – that is to say predicting the unknown – and *backcasting*, which is predicting the known. When evaluating forecast methods it is necessary to know the actual values in order to compute the forecast errors on which comparison depends. Thus forecast evaluation undertaken to improve genuine forecasts always involves backcasting. Genuine forecasts can be evaluated only after events have occurred and data have been published. Herein we will make a genuine forecast that the reader ought to check against the data that will appear in *Travel Trends*, 2001, and will make backcasts for 1998, 1999 and 2000 to evaluate simple objective methods.

Method 1: No change in level

About the simplest objective forecast is to assume no change in the level of the data – that it does not have trends in it – an approach often termed NAÏVE1. This method simply uses the last observation to forecast; 'no change' is the assumption. Thus, the one-step-ahead NAÏVE1 forecast made at period t is:

$$F(t + 1) = A(t)$$

The corresponding two-step-ahead NAÏVE1 forecast made at period t is:

$$(t)F(t + 2) = A(t)$$

and so on.

Now, refer to the annual data on total visits (tourist and others) to the UK by overseas residents presented in Table 6.1. Suppose we wish to estimate the numbers of overseas residents who will visit the UK in 2001 (these data are not yet available in summer 2003 at the time of writing this example). Given that tourist flows into the UK in 2001 were adversely affected by two major unpredictable events (foot and mouth disease and the attacks on Washington and New York) it is likely that the naïve forecast will be more inaccurate than otherwise expected.

NAÏVE1 would forecast 25,209,000 visits based on the value for 2000. To assess the value of this forecast, however, is impossible as we do not have the data for 2001! To avoid the wait, and approximate the actual process of forecasting, implies comparing past forecasts with actual values of demand. One possibility would thus be to construct a set of forecast errors that compared actual values for a particular year with those of the previous year. Thus the error for year 2000 would be the forecast from 1999, 25,394,000 visitors less those actually arriving in 2000 – 25, 209,000 visitors – generating an error of (–)185,000 visitors. This represents an over-prediction of demand. A similar process could be repeated for all years that data are available and RMSE and MAFE computed.

This approach assumes that the forecast is revised each time that data become available and is essentially a continuous one-step-ahead forecast. This issue is broached again below. However, one might

Table 6.1   Visits to the UK by overseas residents, 1976–2000

Year	Visits (thousands)
1976	10,808
1977	12,281
1978	12,646
1979	12,486
1980	12,421
1981	11,452
1982	11,636
1983	12,464
1984	13,644
1985	14,449
1986	13,897
1987	15,566
1988	15,799
1989	17,338
1990	18,013
1991	17,125
1992	18,535
1993	19,863
1994	20,794
1995	23,537
1996	25,163
1997	25,515
1998	25,745
1999	25,394
2000	25,209

Source: ONS (1996) *Travel Trends*, Table 1.1 until 1995; ONS (2000) *Travel Trends*, Table 2.01 thereafter

also be forecasting over longer periods and thus use backcasts to replicate the forecasting period. Table 6.2 produces these for 1998–2000 using data up to and including 1997. This attempts to replicate what a real NAÏVE1 forecaster would have predicted for those years if operating with data available in early 1998. The backcasts, the actual values, the errors and their squares and absolute values are stacked in successive columns.

The fifth row collects sums of the squares and the absolute values of errors, permitting calculation of the RMSFE and MAFE statistics, reported below the table. To simplify notation we continue to use 'F', although as you will appreciate really we are thinking about backcast error. It seems that whichever statistic one looks at one can expect to get an error of about 230,000 visits a year, about 1% of the 20 million or so visits recorded. Incidentally Table 6.2 illustrates why the mean forecast error is hopeless as an index of performance. The relatively dismal under-prediction for 1998 largely cancels out the even worse over-prediction for 2000.

The relevant forecast evaluation statistics are:

- root mean square forecast error = $\sqrt{(161,177/3)}$ = $\sqrt{53,725.7}$ = 232 (rounded)
- mean absolute forecast error = 657/3 = 219

NAÏVE1 is very simple and inexpensive (ignoring the costs of making wrong decisions). Given that visits are thought to display some inertia, it may be a fairly good indicator for a year ahead. But a glance at Table 6.1 suggests the flows tend to grow, so

NAÏVE1 is not likely to work well over longer periods. Nevertheless it serves a useful purpose as a standard that more expensive objective forecasting methods ought to (but cannot always) beat. If they cannot the forecaster should stay with NAÏVE1.

Method 2: No change in growth rate

Another simple objective forecasting method that allows for a trend, as discussed above, is to assume that the series in question will grow (or decline) at a constant proportional rate equal to the most recently observed growth rate. This is often termed NAÏVE2 by forecasters and like NAÏVE1 it sets a standard below which more expensive forecast methods ought not to fall. Clearly constant growth is an assumption barely less simplistic than constant level. To ensure comparability with the last subsection we compute the genuine NAÏVE2 forecast for 2001 and then the 1998–2000 backcasts reported in Table 6.3.

The expression for the genuine one-step-ahead NAÏVE2 forecast made at time t is:

$$F(t + 1) = A(t)\{A(t)/A(t - 1)\}$$

Referring to the data from Table 6.1 this becomes:

$$F(2001) = 25,209\{25,209/25,394) = 25,209\{0.9927\} = 25,025$$

We use the values for 1999 and 2000 to estimate visit numbers in 2001. The genuine NAÏVE2 prediction is that visits will be down by about 200,000 on the 2000 level. By way of some explanation the expression in {} is the ratio of visits

Table 6.2 NAÏVE1 forecast performance, 1998–2000

Year	Forecast (thousands)	Actual (thousands)	(F – A)	(F A)²	IF – AI
1998	25,515	25,745	−230	52,900	230
1999	25,515	25,394	121	14,641	121
2000	25,515	25,209	306	93,636	306
Σ				161,177	657

Source: ONS (1996) *Travel Trends*, Table 1.1; ONS (2000) *Travel Trends*, Table 2.01

in 2000 to visits in 1999 giving a numerical value of 0.9927. It estimates the proportional growth rate between 1999 and 2000. This is then multiplied by the actual value of visits in 2000 to scale the value up or down. Of course, the latter applies in this case. As it is smaller than 1 we immediately infer that visits fell. The numerical value suggests they fell by about 0.73%. The ratio of visits must be positive – if it is negative there is a mistake. A number bigger than 1 indicates positive growth. Given that visits tended to grow over the sample period one would not want to use a negative growth rate to extrapolate beyond 2001. One way around this is to average previous growth rates instead of using one year's unrepresentative negative growth.

Using this approach one can compute NAÏVE2 backcasts covering the years 1998–2000. The appropriate formulae are:

$$F(1998) = A(1997)\{A(1997)/A(1996)\} = 25,515\{25,515/25,163\}$$

$$= 25,515\{1.014\} = 25,872 \text{ (rounded)}$$

From which it is apparent that overseas visits to the UK grew by about 1.4% between 1996 and 1997. Applying the rules of compound interest the backcasts for 1999 and 2000 are respectively

$$\text{Year 1999 backcast} = 25,515\,(1.014)^2 = 26,234 \text{ (rounded)}$$

and

$$\text{Year 2000 backcast} = 25,515\,(1.014)^3 = 26,601 \text{ (rounded)}$$

These and their associated errors are presented in Table 6.3 in the same format as Table 6.2 to facilitate comparison with the NAÏVE1 backcasts.

The relevant forecast evaluation statistics are:

- root mean square forecast error = $\sqrt{(2,659,393/3)} = \sqrt{886,464} = 942$ (rounded)
- mean absolute forecast error = $2,359/3 = 786$ (rounded).

NAÏVE1 in this instance is better than NAÏVE2 when comparing Tables 6.2 and 6.3, whether one uses RMSFE or MAFE as a criterion. The latter is expected to produce forecast errors about four times bigger in relation to the approximately 20 million annual visits by people from overseas. Regarding the direction of change, NAÏVE2 predicts two successive increases in visits, whereas actual visits drop in both periods. NAÏVE1, because it posits no change, does poorly, but better than NAÏVE2. When visits are falling it is better to have forecast no change than an increase.

It would not be difficult to produce a better set of NAÏVE2 backcasts based on some other growth rate. Practising forecasters would explore variations on each type of forecasting method in the hope of discovering the 'best' versions of each and determining which was the best overall. In this chapter no attempt is made to search out the best method for these data; it aims merely to introduce some forecasting methods and apply simple evaluation criteria to them. Like NAÏVE1, NAÏVE2 is useful in setting a standard that more expensive forecasts must be shown to beat if it is to be worth making them.

Table 6.3 NAÏVE2 forecast performance, 1998–2000

Year	Forecast (thousands)	Actual (thousands)	(F – A)	(F – A)²	IF – AI
1998	25,872	25,745	127	16,129	127
1999	26,234	25,394	840	705,600	840
2000	26,601	25,209	1,392	1,937,664	1,392
Σ				2,659,393	2,359

Source: ONS (1996) *Travel Trends*, Table 1.1; ONS (2000) *Travel Trends*, Table 2.01

Table 6.4 Quarterly visits to the UK by overseas residents, 1993–2000

Period	Actual (thousands)	MA4 (thousands)	MAC4 (thouands)	SR
1993/1	3,611	–	–	–
1993/2	5,222	–	–	–
1993/3	6,698	4,966	4,995	1.341
1993/4	4,332	5,023	5,029	0.861
1994/1	3,841	5,035	5,060	0.759
1994/2	5,269	5,084	5,142	1.025
1994/3	6,892	5,199	5,246	1.314
1994/4	4,792	5,292	5,378	0.891
1995/1	4,216	5,463	5,570	0.757
1995/2	5,952	5,676	5,780	1.030
1995/3	7,746	5,884	5,947	1.303
1995/4	5,623	6,010	6,101	0.922
1996/1	4,719	6,192	6,241	0.756
1996/2	6,680	6,289	6,290	1.062
1996/3	8,132	6,291	6,319	1.287
1996/4	5,632	6,346	6,317	0.892
1997/1	4,940	6,288	6,293	0.785
1997/2	6,447	6,297	6,338	1.017
1997/3	8,168	6,379	6,363	1.284
1997/4	5,961	6,346	6,394	0.932
1998/1	4,804	6,442	6,425	0.748
1998/2	6,834	6,407	6,422	1.064
1998/3	8,027	6,436	6,467	1.241
1998/4	6,080	6,497	6,493	0.936
1991/1	5,046	6,488	6,474	0.779
1999/2	6,799	6,460	6,405	1.062
1999/3	7,913	6,349	6,342	1.248
1999/4	5,636	6,335	6,327	0.891
2000/1	4,993	6,319	6,323	0.790
2000/2	6,733	6,326	6,314	1.066
2000/3	7,943	6,302	–	–
2000/4	5,540	–	–	–

Source: ONS (1997) *Travel Trends*, Table 3.01; ONS (2000) *Travel Trends*, Table 2.01

It should be remembered that in these sections we investigated backcasting power over a three-year horizon – as if forecasts are made and no further action is taken for three years. In reality all available information would be accounted for. In this case, as implied in the discussion of NAÏVE1, forecasts would be updated as data become available. Finally, other simple approaches might involve some form of averaging process. The moving average method is applied in the next section to investigate seasonality.

Method 3: Decomposition of series

Many economic series that appear at quarterly or monthly intervals may be broken down into the following components:

- trend (T) – represents the long-run tendency, assumed to be approximately linear growth or decline
- cyclical (C) – represents recurrent fluctuations, usually of about three to four years, in business activity
- seasonal (S) – fluctuations that apply within the year
- irregular (I) – captures unpredictable events, for example unusually severe weather or terrorist attacks in places considered previously safe.

Annual data are more simply handled as the seasonal element is averaged out. But since holiday-makers' decisions are heavily dependent on their expectations about the weather, whether they are heading for the beach or the ski slope, the seasonal factor should not be ignored. A firm may be interested mainly in forecasting the original series, complete with seasonality and additionally in forecasting the 'seasonally adjusted' series – that is to say with S and I deleted.

Sticking with the data on visits by overseas residents to the UK, the second column of Table 6.4 stacks quarterly observations of the number of visits to the UK by overseas residents from 1993 through 2000. The data are taken from the International Passenger Survey. It is apparent that the second and third quarter flows typically exceed the average. A marginal point to bear in mind is that monthly or (better still) weekly data would pinpoint peaks and troughs more precisely.

The analyst seeks to decompose the (say) quarterly series into its components and construct forecasts that either remove (seasonally adjusted) or embody (actual) seasonality. There are several ways to decompose a series, one of the simpler methods being 'ratio to moving average', which assumes a multiplicative relationship between the components that make up the actual series:

$$A(t) = T(t) \times C(t) \times S(t) \times I(t)$$

The first step is to construct a moving average of observations (four-period for quarterly data and 12-period for monthly data) to approximate the trend and cyclical components.[2] A four-period moving average (MA4) is simply the average of four successive quarterly values, representing the trend and cyclical components at period t. Each value of MA4 contains observations dated in all seasons, tending to cancel out seasonal effects. Averaging also tends to remove the irregular component on the further assumption that its average value is 0. Note that to base the moving average on period t you need data about subsequent as well as prior periods. Thus one can define MA4(t) in the following way:

$$MA4(t) = 0.25\{A(t + 1) + A(t) + A(t - 1) + A(t - 2)\}$$

The third column of Table 6.4 stacks a four-period moving average precisely as defined above. As four is an even number MA4(t) is not centred on period t, but on the interval between periods t and t − 1. Check that the first observation (4,966) of MA4 in Table 6.6 is simply the sum of the four quarterly values for 1993 divided by four and rounded to the nearest whole number; 4,966 is centred on the interval between the second and third quarters of 1993. To obtain a moving average centred on period

t one might consider another four-period moving average MA4*(t) that looks forward one period in the sense that its value is centred between period t and period t + 1. In this case

$$MA4*(t) =$$
$$0.25\{A(t + 2) + A(t + 1) + A(t) + A(t - 1)\}$$

Inspection shows that MA4* is simply MA4 with all the actual values taken forward one period. Since MA4* is centred on the interval between periods t and t + 1, the average of MA4 and MA4* (MAC4) is a four-period moving average of A centred on period t. Thus

$$MAC4(t) = 0.5\{MA4(t) + MA4*(t)\}$$

MAC4 is the index of the trend and cyclical components used herein. It appears in the fourth column of Table 6.4. Check that the first observation of MAC4 is the average of the current and one period lagged values of MA4.

Dividing actual visits A by MAC4 yields estimates of the seasonal ratios (SR). These record whether visits during a given quarter tend to exceed or fall below trend. A value of SR above unity indicates a quarter with above-average visit numbers, for example the third for visitors to the UK. The fifth column of Table 6.4 holds the computed seasonal ratios for the sample period. Thus

$$A(t)/MAC4(t) = S(t) \times I(t) \equiv SR(t)$$

Given a run of data over several years the calculated values of SR may be averaged to provide a better estimate of the 'true' value than may be expected from one observation. Averaging tends to remove the influence of irregular events further, assuming these tend to equal 0. The averages are the raw seasonal factors (RSF) stored in the final column of Table 6.5. The expression 'raw' indicates that they are unlikely to add to 4, and require to be adjusted to do so. In the sample they sum to 4.007. If not adjusted our forecasts would systematically over-predict. We are unable to avoid errors resulting from random events, but we should not knowingly embody systematic (avoidable) errors. The adjusted seasonal factors are used to remove and to restore seasonality to the data.

2 If one was confident that cycles averaged (say) three years peak to peak one might construct a twelve-quarter moving average to remove the cyclical effects, but cycles are imperfectly regular. Another disadvantage of a longer moving average is that to centre it on the current period requires knowledge of periods further into the future and into the past than is the case with a short moving average. We stick with four periods in the example, losing two observations at the beginning and another two at the end (compare the original visit data in Table 6.6 with those for MAC4).

Table 6.5   Seasonal ratios and raw seasonal factors, 1993–1998

Quarter	1993	1994	1995	1996	1997	1998	RSF
1	–	0.759	0.757	0.756	0.785	0.748	0.761
2	–	1.025	1.030	1.062	1.017	1.064	1.040
3	1.341	1.314	1.303	1.287	1.284	–	1.306
4	0.861	0.891	0.922	0.892	0.932	–	0.900
Σ							4.007

Source: previous Table 6.4

'Why 4?' you may ask. Assume there is no seasonal variation – that the actual value and MAC4 are always equal. In that case each raw seasonal factor is unity and given there are four seasons, the sum of four units is four. Whatever the seasonal variation relative to MAC4 the seasonal factors must add to 4. If the raw estimates do not, they require to be amended. To obtain the adjusted seasonal factors (ASF) required in subsequent analysis the raw seasonal factor for a given quarter must be first quadrupled, and then divided by the sum of all four raw factors.

Adjusted seasonal factors are presented in Table 6.6, computed from the SR data in Table 6.4 up to 1998 second quarter, the reason being to preserve the 1999 and 2000 visits data for a trend, cyclical, seasonal, irregular (TCSI) backcast. Every computed SR in Table 6.4 depends on knowing visits two quarters ahead. If our backcasts are to replicate what a genuine forecaster in very early 1999 might have produced, it is vital to ensure as far as possible that we use only information that was then available. The situation facing a genuine forecaster in early 2001 is very different. Once again, such a forecaster is permitted (indeed expected) to make use of all information available.

Given the estimated ASFs we can produce seasonally adjusted visits (SAV) from the actual numbers. To do so, divide each actual observation by the appropriate adjusted seasonal factor. The original and the seasonally adjusted series are shown in the second and fourth columns of Table 6.7. We may extrapolate backwards and forwards to estimate the four values lost when constructing MAC4. Figures in the SAV column are rounded to the nearest thousand.

Backcasting and forecasting SAV might be done using moving averages. Given a forecast of SAV in some future period, it is necessary only to multiply it by the relevant ASF to arrive at the forecast of the actual value of visits. This operation may be reversed to obtain a forecast of seasonally adjusted visits from a forecast of actual visits. Various lengths of moving average may be tried to determine which provides the best (perhaps in an RMSFE or directional sense) backcasts. There is no guarantee that a particular moving average will always forecast best.

Purely for illustrative purposes we compare backcasts using first-order and fourth-order moving averages of SAV. If looking for the best order moving average one might examine every one up to about six. The first-order moving average is simply the previous period's SAV – this model being a close relative of NAÏVE1.

Table 6.6   Raw and adjusted seasonal factors, 1993–1998

Quarter	RSF	ASF
1	0.761	0.760
2	1.040	1.038
3	1.306	1.304
4	0.900	0.898
Σ	4.007	4.000

Source: previous Table 6.5

Thus the first-order moving average forecast is:

$$F(t + 1) = SAV(t)$$

And the fourth-order (four-period) moving average forecast is of course:

$$F(t + 1) =$$
$$0.25\{SAV(t) + SAV(t - 1) + SAV(t - 2) + SAV(t - 3)\}$$

We backcast seasonally adjusted visits through 1999 and 2000. In effect we attempt to replicate the forecasts that could have been made in early 1999 by anybody using our method and data. Backcasts, their errors and squares are stored in the columns of Table 6.8. Sums of squares are reported in the last row. SAVL denotes the backcast made using one period lagged SAV while SAV4 indicates the backcast made when using the four-period moving average. SAV4 performs better, both on RMSFE and MAFE criteria. The mean absolute error is about 3% of the level of the variable being backcast. Both methods wrongly predict the direction of change in SAV three times.

The relevant forecast evaluation statistics for the one-period version are:

- root mean square forecast error = $\sqrt{(557,156/8)}$ = 264 (rounded)
- mean absolute error = 1,762/8 = 220 (rounded).

The relevant forecast evaluation statistics for the four-period version are:

- root mean square forecast error = $\sqrt{(497,847/8)}$ = 249 (rounded)
- mean absolute error = 1,739/8 = 217 (rounded).

A firm may be more interested in estimating how many visits will occur in a quarter, rather than the general trend. This requires converting the data into unadjusted form and using them to predict actual visits. Backcasting proceeds in a similar way. First the forecaster derives a visits series with the seasonal variation restored. We already have the necessary information: the adjusted series SAV in Table 6.7 and the estimated seasonal factors (adjusted to prevent inflation and deflation of numbers) in Table 6.6.

Table 6.7 Actual and seasonally adjusted visits to the UK, 1993–2000

Period	Actual (thousands)	ASF (thousands)	SAV
1993/1	3,611	0.760	4,751
1993/2	5,222	1.038	5,031
1993/3	6,698	1.304	5,137
1993/4	4,332	0.898	4,824
1994/1	3,841	0.760	5,054
1994/2	5,269	1.038	5,076
1994/3	6,892	1.304	5,285
1994/4	4,792	0.898	5,336
1995/1	4,216	0.760	5,547
1995/2	5,952	1.038	5,734
1995/3	7,746	1.304	5,940
1995/4	5,623	0.898	6,262
1996/1	4,719	0.760	6,209
1996/2	6,680	1.038	6,435
1996/3	8,132	1.304	6,236
1996/4	5,632	0.898	6,272
1997/1	4,940	0.760	6,500
1997/2	6,447	1.038	6,211
1997/3	8,168	1.304	6,264
1997/4	5,961	0.898	6,638
1998/1	4,804	0.760	6.321
1998/2	6,834	1.038	6,584
1998/3	8,027	1.304	6,156
1998/4	6,080	0.898	6,771
1999/1	5,046	0.760	6,639
1999/2	6,799	1.038	6,550
1999/3	7,913	1.304	6,068
1999/4	5,636	0.898	6,276
2000/1	4,993	0.760	6,570
2000/2	6,733	1.038	6,487
2000/3	7,943	1.304	6,091
2000/4	5,540	0.898	6,169

Source: previous Tables 6.4 and 6.6

Table 6.8   SAV, backcasts, their errors and squared errors, 1999–2000

Period	SAV	SAVL	SAVLE	SAVLE^2	SAV4	SAV4E	SAV4E^2
1999/1	6,639	6,771	132	17,424	6,458	−181	32,761
1999/2	6,550	6,639	89	7,921	6,538	−12	144
1999/3	6,068	6,550	482	232,324	6,529	461	212,521
1999/4	6,276	6,068	−208	43,264	6,507	231	53,361
2000/1	6,570	6,276	−294	86,436	6,383	−187	34,969
2000/2	6,487	6,570	83	6,889	6,366	−121	14,641
2000/3	6,091	6,487	396	156,816	6,350	259	67,081
2000/4	6,199	6,091	−78	6,084	6,356	287	82,369
Σ				557,156			497,841

Source: previous Table 6.7

Divide each SAV observation by the appropriate ASF to obtain the unadjusted series. Various moving averages of the resulting series may be used in backcasting to try to establish the best forecasting model. Provided the seasonal pattern is very regular, the best model for seasonally adjusted data will probably be the best for unadjusted data.

Method 4: Autoregression

NAÏVE1 limits us to construct forecast equations that attach weights of 0 (if not used) or 1 (if used) to past observations of the variable we want to forecast and NAÏVE2 is similarly restrictive. Four-period moving averages as applied above limit us to applying weights of 0.25 or 0. Better forecasts might result if these weights could take on a wider range of values. Rather than NAÏVE1, one might specify a looser but closely related model that also uses today's value to predict tomorrow's, but that does not so restrict the values of the weights. Such a formula might be:

$$F(t) = a + bA(t - 1)$$

As discussed in Chapter 4, the terms a and b are unknown parameters (assumed constant during the sampling period) to be estimated by the forecaster and used to predict A beyond the sample period. Estimation can proceed using an appropriate

computer package that has, for example, linear regression options. Standardised packages such as Excel and SPSS and dedicated econometric packages could be used. Specifically b is the 'weight' to be attached to last year's visits. While NAÏVE1 assumes a = 0 and b = 1, the equation above permits a and b to take on many values.

Given that in general the forecasts are not known it is impossible to estimate a and b directly. However, it is possible to investigate past visits data to estimate the closely related equation:

$$A(t) = a + bA(t - 1) + v(t)$$

This is a simple first-order autoregressive (AR1) model. 'Autoregressive' means that the variable is forecast using information about its own past values – like the other naïve methods. 'First order' means that one lagged value only is incorporated. Here v is an error term introduced to allow for the inevitable errors in observation and the innate unpredictability of life. The simplest regression procedure 'ordinary least squares' permits the researcher to estimate a and b to minimise the sum of squared distances between the original observations and the corresponding points on the regression line. Obviously the smaller that sum, the more closely the fitted equation and the data agree.

The sum of squared residuals must not be confused with the sum of squared forecast errors – no forecasts are involved. It is not even a test of backcasting power, since all the data have been used to estimate the equation. Backcasting requires the investigator to preserve some observations. Thus the forecaster can divide the sample into a 'fitting period', which provides data to estimate a and b, and a 'backcasting period', which provides data for the tests. In this chapter an estimate of an AR1 equation using data to 1997 is presented. Data from 1998 to 2000 are preserved for backcasting, thus making a comparison possible with the earlier NAÏVE1 and NAÏVE2 backcasts.

The simple AR1 model for annual visits is a wholly pedagogic device. The econometrics package Microfit is used to estimate the equation from 1977 (one period is lost to set up a lag) to 1997, preserving 1998–2000 for tests as explained above. The estimated AR1 model (coefficient estimates are rounded to two places of decimals) is:

$$A(t) = -188.38 + 1.06A(t-1) + \text{residual } (t)$$

Given the space constraints and limited pedagogic aims we pay small attention to the diagnostic statistics. Suffice it to say that the estimates of a and b are not significantly different from 0 and 1 respectively. Also – of which more later – the estimate of b suggests that other things equal visits grow by about 6% annually.

Microfit provides a push-button forecasting option that generates the forecast (backcast), the associated errors and the sums of their squares and of their absolute values. This is a 'dynamic' forecast, which means that forecast visits in (say) 1998 are used to forecast 1999 visits – as opposed to 'static' forecasts that use actual values as forecasts. Dynamic forecasts are closer to real forecasting, where future values cannot be used as they are unknown.

The AR1 dynamic forecast corresponds fairly closely to the three-year-ahead forecasts made using NAÏVE1 and NAÏVE2 reported in Tables 6.2 and 6.3. Table 6.9 holds the dynamic forecasts, the actual values, the errors, their squares and absolute values and the relevant sums. Clearly on both the RMSFE and MAFE criteria AR1 predicts much less well than either NAÏVE1 or NAÏVE2 up to three periods ahead. Like NAÏVE2, AR1 forecasts successive increases in visits in a period when the totals fell every year.

The relevant forecast evaluation statistics are:

- root mean square forecast error = $\sqrt{(30,559,099/3)} = \sqrt{10,186,366.3} = 3,192$
- mean absolute forecast error = $8,581/3 = 2,860$ (rounded)

One does not have to look too far to see the reason for this poor performance. An arbitrary equation was adopted for estimation and forecasting. In practice more complicated autoregressions might be used. For example, of a higher order, perhaps the second order AR2 process given by the equation:

$$F(t) = a + bA(t-1) + cA(t-2)$$

Thus autoregressions of varying order may be estimated, their backcast errors computed and tests conducted to identify the preferred autoregressive form.

Table 6.9 AR1 dynamic forecasts of overseas visits, 1998–2000

Year	Forecast (F) (thousands)	Actual (A) (thousands)	(F – A)	(F – A)²		F – A	
1998	26,858	25,745	1,113	1,238,769	1,113
1999	28,281	25,394	2,887	8,334,769	2,887
2000	29,790	25,209	4,581	20,985,561	4,581
Σ				26,577,745	8,581

Source: ONS (2000) *Travel Trends*, Table 2.01
Estimates produced by Microfit 4.0

More generally, as implied in Chapter 5, regression procedures and their associated hypothesis tests when applied to time-series data are applicable strictly to data that are 'stationary' – that have constant means and variances. The visits data appear to violate these conditions as the mean trends upward over time – as the regression estimate of b indicates. One should test that data is stationary before estimating a forecasting equation. This is a fairly complex issue. In general terms the test, known as a unit root test, involves an autoregression of the form:

$$A(t) = \alpha + \beta A(t - 1) + u(t)$$

Here u(t) is a random influence with constant mean and variance. Using modified statistical tables a unit root test assesses whether or not $\beta = 1$ or $\beta < 1$. If it is the former then A(t) will be non-stationary. In this case one could construct another data series given as:

$$\Delta A(t) = A(t) - A(t - 1) = u(t)$$

By definition of u(t) this would be stationary. This differencing of the data produced an equation in which changes in the variable of interest could be analysed reliably if not the levels directly. Levels could be derived from adding changes to previous levels. In the language of the forecaster, A(t) is integrated of order 1 because a first difference can produce a stationary series. Of course, if $\beta < 1$ then one could estimate the relationship describing the levels directly.

This discussion suggests the possible application of the autoregressive integrated moving average (ARIMA) approach to modelling visits. This approach combines the idea that one can forecast from an autoregressive process, with the need to difference data, to the idea that the 'random' terms might also follow a moving average pattern. The equation

$$\Delta A(t) = \delta \Delta A(t - 1) + u(t) + \theta u(t - 1)$$

is an example of a (1, 1, 1) process. In order, the numbers imply that the equation is autoregressive of order '1', that a first difference is stationary and that the random terms comprise a '1' period moving average. In principle all these possibilities can vary. It is clear that though sophisticated this approach has two not inconsiderable disadvantages. First it requires highly skilled labour and second (more problematic in the actual circumstances) very long runs of data. The method thus tends to dominate forecasting in financial markets where daily, hourly or real-time data are regularly available as opposed to markets involving real goods and services. It remains, however, that simple versions may be useful.

Advantages and disadvantages of various methods

By definition we arrive at purely objective forecasts by processes that are knowable, thus in principle anybody can be trained in objective forecasting. This is by no means true of subjective forecasting that purely draws on opinion. This fact does not by itself imply that objective forecasts are generally preferable. First, subjective forecasts are frequently more accurate and not necessarily more expensive to produce. Second, there are very few purely objective forecasts – at any rate among those published.

Forecasters are seldom willing to put the latest data into a computer and accept what emerges. The reason is quite simple – the first set of numbers may look (and sometimes does) unbelievable. Should this happen the forecaster will apply a 'fix' and rerun the programme (more 'fixes' may be needed) until a more acceptable result is obtained. Hence forecasts that at first glance appear to be objective are often in part subjective.

Regression-based forecasts also permit one to estimate the range of uncertainty surrounding them through diagnostic testing, although standard test statistics are not necessarily applicable, for instance when the data are not stationary. Moreover, long runs of data might be needed. It remains, however, that it is hard to estimate a range of uncertainty around a subjective forecast, beyond conjecturing 'most optimistic' and 'least optimistic' outcomes.

Combining forecasts

It was argued earlier that there are many ways to forecast, that many forecasts are made available virtually free of charge and that a firm may buy industry-specific forecasts from providers or generate its own. The opportunity cost of staff time may make this more expensive than buying a forecast, although a firm that already has a large forecasting function might consider selling its services to other businesses. No one forecasting method always or even 'nearly always' dominates the others on all or most selection criteria.

This suggests that the firm ought to consider combining forecasts, hoping that when some are over-estimating others will be under-estimating and the average might come closer to the truth than even the 'best' individual forecast does. Similarly investors in unit trusts spread their risks across industries and countries in the expectation of securing a safer return than they might obtain on a single company. Combining forecasts in the simplest case might amount to no more than calculating an average. Averaging might weigh each individual forecast according to the degree of 'faith' the user attaches to it, perhaps informed by its previous forecast errors. So many forecasts are made it is not likely the firm ever has (or needs) them all.

But averaging is an inefficient way to combine forecasts since it ignores the assumptions that lie behind them. The most intelligent way to combine forecasts is to inquire into how they are arrived at, whether the assumptions on which they depend seem credible, and to make an informed decision on the basis of the best information (including how to interpret forecasts) available. A forecast that looks incredible might be ignored on the (dubious) assumption that the majority is usually right. Occasionally the majority is wrong.

Whether combining forecasts is worthwhile depends on how independent they are. The more they agree, the less the potential for gain. Ultimately whether it is worth combining two forecasts depends on the information sets from which they were derived. The more independent the data (other things being equal) the more beneficial is combination.

If both come largely from the same data set, as is the case with published UK macro-economic models, the potential for gain is limited, although not necessarily insignificant. If one forecast of UK outward tourist flows in 2003 emerges from a study (like MINTEL) of participants in 2000, while the other emerges from a study (like the General Household Survey) of participants and non-participants alike in 2000, their combination might be profitable.

Finally it cannot have escaped the reader's notice that the combination of forecasts – like the subsequent taking of avoiding action – belongs more to the subjective than the objective sphere. Which forecasts to survey, which to combine (and why) and how (indeed whether) to combine them are all decisions dependent in varying degrees on subjective judgement.

Conclusions

Forecasting is fascinating to academics, but vital to business. It is easy to make a forecast but very difficult to make a good one. There is a multiplicity of forecasting methods from which to choose and of criteria to help one do so; similarly there is much information of which the firm may or may not be aware. A firm that is interested in forecasting must judge which information and which methods to deploy and how to combine them. It also needs to monitor progress in its forecasting activity and to react sensibly to changing information. This is above all within the realm of subjective as opposed to objective judgement. Some appreciation of the inter-related tourism markets and how they relate to the wider national and global economies is required.

7 Forecasting consumer expenditure on leisure

Professor Chris Gratton and Themis Kokolakakis Leisure Industries Research Centre, Sheffield Hallam University

Focus questions

- What are the main factors affecting consumer spending on leisure?
- How are leisure markets defined?
- What are the key elements in forecasting leisure markets?
- What is the difference between 'home' and 'away' leisure?

- What are the key short-run and long-run determinants of leisure consumption?
- What lessons can be learned from forecasting experience?

Introduction

This chapter illustrates how secondary data can be used for the analysis and forecasting of consumer expenditure on leisure. The current authors prepare such forecasts for annual publication in the publication *Leisure Forecasts*. This was first published in 1982 by Bill Martin and Sandra Mason of Leisure Consultants Ltd, which was taken over by the Leisure Industries Research Centre (LIRC) in the mid-1990s. Before publishing *Leisure Forecasts* Martin and Mason had produced similar forecasts for the Henley Centre for Forecasting since the mid-1970s. Although the forecasting models and the databases LIRC uses are updated annually, LIRC still essentially employs the same methods as Martin and Mason did in the mid-1970s.

This chapter is divided into four main sections. In the first section we outline the basic approach used to produce forecasts and analyse the main factors affecting consumer expenditure on leisure and how they have changed over the last 25 years of the last century. The second section discusses how we define the leisure market and its various subsectors, and analyse the relative sizes of these subsectors. The third section gives an overview of the output of the

forecasting models produced in early 2002 for the forecast period 2002–6. The final section looks back over the 1975–2000 period and the lessons learned in relation to forecasting leisure expenditures by ourselves and Martin and Mason.

Main factors affecting the leisure market

LIRC forecasts each sector of the leisure market separately. The starting point is forecasting the long-term behaviour of consumption in the economy as a whole. The underlying assumption is that spending in each leisure sector is closely related to the movement in overall consumer spending. The relationship between the two is specified as the combination of the two elements noted in Table 7.1.

The methodology is designed to provide a formal basis for modelling, and for incorporating underlying leisure influences, in circumstances where the data are, in most cases, inadequate to permit formal regression analyses such as those discussed in Chapters 4, 5 and 6. Forecasts are made separately of sector spending at constant prices and specific price indices for each sector. These forecasts are then combined to produce the forecast for sector spending at current prices. For some sectors this system is not used. Instead, spending forecasts are derived from more detailed models that relate trends in sector volume (units) to spending. Sectors where this approach is used include television and most other media, and sightseeing.

The most important sources of leisure-related data, provided by the ONS, are the publications *Consumer Trends*, *Family Spending*, *Travel Trends* and *Living in Britain: Results from the General Household Survey*. A detailed picture of leisure spending can be constructed from *Consumer Trends* and *Family Spending*. Other official publications used are: *Social Trends*, *UK National Accounts*, *Sector Review: Catering and Allied Trades*, *Sector Review: Retailing*, *Sector Review: Service Trades*, *Producer Price Indices* (MM22), *Labour Market Trends*, *New Earnings Survey*, *Population Trends* and *Focus on Personal Travel*.

Thus, by way of review, LIRC assumes that three major factors influence leisure behaviour over the long-term:

- the availability of leisure time
- the rate of growth of the economy (or consumers' incomes)
- technology.

We review below how these factors have changed since 1975 by drawing on the data sources noted above.

Availability of leisure time

As discussed in Chapter 4, a key component of sports, leisure and tourism demand is the availability of time. In 1975, it was relatively easy to predict the long-term trend in the availability of leisure time. It had been declining throughout the 20th century and certainly over the post-war period. The future then was clear: it would continue to decline through the forecast period to 2000. This is certainly what happened in every other European country. But it did not happen in Britain. Between 1975 and 1984 working hours fell for full-time employees. This downward trend was so significant during this period that the average working day fell by around one hour per day. By 1985, full-time male workers were working an average of 40.3 hours per week.

However, 1985 signalled the end of the post-war trend of a decline in working hours in Britain. By 1989 the average working week for full-time male workers had increased to 44.1 hours. The rate at which working hours for men was increasing slowed in the early 1990s, so that it had increased to 46.8 hours per week for male full-time employees by 1995, which is higher than the figure for 1975. Full-time female employees' hours also reached a low point in 1985 at 38.5 hours per week. They had reached 39.7 hours by 1995. In addition to longer working hours, time budget studies show that there has also been sharp increases the amount of time spent on household duties such as shopping, on domestic travel and on childcare since 1975. All of these reduce the amount of time available for leisure.

Rise in consumers' incomes

Consumers' incomes had virtually doubled in real terms over the post-war period up to 1975. Household incomes grew even faster as more and more married women entered the workforce. Although the post-war economy had tended to grow and then decline, following a relatively short economic cycle, the long-term trend was definitely upwards and it was reasonably safe to predict long-term growth at a rate of 2% to 2.5% per annum. As it turned out, the cyclical swings between 1975 and 1992 proved to be even sharper than the previous 25 years with deep recessions in 1980–2 and 1990–2, and a huge consumer boom in the mid to late 1980s. Since 1992, the British economy has experienced its steadiest, most controlled growth path in the whole of the post-war period, making long-term forecasting much more straightforward, if it could be sustained. However, few economic forecasters would be prepared to suggest that we have seen an end, just yet, to the rollercoaster ride that has typified the performance of the British economy in the past. (See *Consumer Trends* and *Economic Trends*.)

Technology

The third factor that we have identified as a major influence on leisure is technology. Two of the most important technical innovations that shaped people's leisure activities in the post-war period were television and the car. Watching television was easily the most popular leisure activity by 1975, with over 98% of people in Britain recording participation in this activity. Ownership of a car was also the prime determinant of out-of-home leisure activities. A third important influence on leisure participation was the relative cheapness of air travel, and the ease with which it could be undertaken, which made travel abroad available to a large proportion of the British population by 1975. One area that would have been difficult, or impossible to predict in 1975, however, would have been the influence that advances in micro electronics would have on the availability of consumer electronic leisure goods. In 1975, the Walkman, CD players, videos, PCs, camcorders, and Sony Playstations were products that nobody had or wanted since they were not available. Yet once they existed, the markets for these products grew at the fastest rate of any of the leisure markets for many years after the product was introduced. This creates the largest problem for long-term leisure forecasting. How can we forecast the market for a product that has not yet been invented but a product that everyone will want, once it is invented? There will always be an important part of leisure behaviour that is driven by new technology. Exactly what that behaviour will be is almost impossible to forecast. (See *The General Household Survey* and *Travel Trends*.)

Short-term influences on leisure markets

Although the three factors above are the main long-term influences on leisure markets, LIRC's models show that year-on-year changes in consumer expenditure on leisure are much more influenced by the state of the economy and the availability of new products on the market normally introduced as the direct result of new technology. Thus when forecasting the year ahead we need to take account of predictions for the rate of growth of GDP, the level of interest rates, changes in disposable incomes, and unemployment, as well as surveying product innovation across the sector. (Data on these are available from the Treasury's *Forecasts for the UK Economy*.)

Distribution of leisure expenditure

From the discussion above it would seem that leisure expenditure will be dominated by those with the most time and money, as discussed in Chapter 4. In reality, only a small minority of the population have an abundance of both. In general, those with the most money are in work, increasingly with partners that are also in full-time employment. Although such two-earner households, particularly when earners are in professional jobs, have seen their household incomes grow at the fastest rates over the last 20 years they have also suffered most from the effects of longer working hours and reduced leisure time. Table 7.1 shows how these households, though 'money rich', are increasingly 'leisure-time poor'. In contrast, the unemployed and many part-time workers are 'leisure-time rich' but 'money poor'. The group that are both time rich and money rich are the affluent retired who have played an increasing role in the leisure market in the recent past. However, there are real worries over whether this group will continue to expand as we move through the 21st century. Inadequate pension provision may mean that people may have to work for longer to obtain an adequate pension in retirement or alternatively to reduce their income on retirement substantially. The tendency for earlier retirement in the 1980s and 1990s is likely therefore to be

Table 7.1 Who has the time and the money?

	Leisure-time rich	Leisure-time poor
Money rich	Affluent retired – especially in 50s and 60s	Full-time core workers – especially executive levels
Money poor	Many part-time workers	Working mothers in poor families
	Unemployed – especially young and long term	Single parents with large families

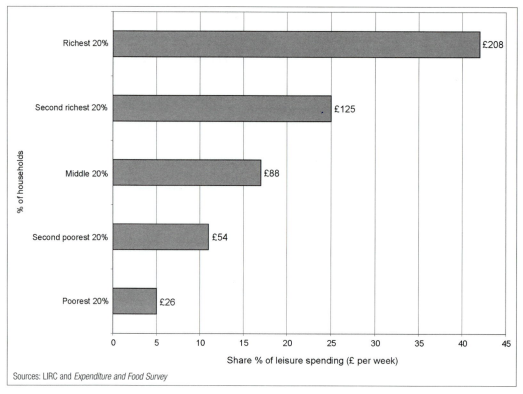

Figure 7.1   The distribution of leisure expenditure, 2002

reversed in the early part of the 21st century, reducing the size of the time and money rich group.

Figure 7.1 shows that being leisure-time poor does not reduce expenditure on leisure. The figure shows that over 40% of total leisure expenditure is accounted for by the richest 20% of households whereas the poorest 20% of households account for less than 5% of total leisure expenditure. Overall the richest 40% of households account for more than two-thirds of all leisure expenditure. Often time constraints on this group lead to households trading time against money, for instance by having several expensive short holidays each year rather than one long holiday.

Defining the leisure market

The Leisure Industries Research Centre classifies the leisure market into two main areas: 'leisure in the home' and 'leisure away from home'.

'Leisure in the home' consists of:

- reading (books, magazines and newspapers)
- home entertainment (television; video and audio equipment; CDs, records and tapes; and PCs)
- house and garden (DIY and gardening)
- hobbies and pastimes (photography, toys and games, and pets).

'Leisure away from home' consists of:

- eating and drinking (eating out, beer, wine and cider, and spirits)
- neighbourhood leisure (active sport, gambling and local entertainment – including cinema, live arts, spectator sports and dancing)
- holidays and tourism (sightseeing, holidays in UK, holidays overseas and foreign tourism).

Data on these sectors are available from *Consumer Trends, Family Spending, The General Household Survey, Travel Trends* and *UK Tourist Statistics*.

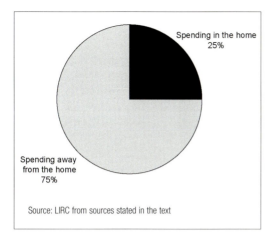

Source: LIRC from sources stated in the text

Figure 7.2   Consumer spending on leisure in the UK, 2002

Figure 7.2 shows that consumer spending on leisure is dominated by away from home leisure spending, which accounts for 75% of the total leisure market in the UK in 2002.

Figure 7.3 shows that within home leisure spending on home entertainment accounts for 39% of the total expenditure, closely followed by spending on house and garden (29%). The smaller sectors are hobbies and pastimes (17%) and reading (15%). Figure 7.4 shows that within away from home leisure spending the eating and drinking sector dominates, accounting for 54% of total away from home leisure spending, with holidays and tourism accounting for a further 31%, the remaining 15% being expenditure on neighbourhood leisure.

Forecasting consumer expenditure in leisure 2002–2006

In this section we outline the outcome of a specific run of the forecasting models. In this case the forecast period is 2002–6 and the exercise was carried out in spring 2002, making 2002 the first forecast year. At the time the exercise was carried out data were available for 2001 and the first part of the exercise is to review leisure spending in that latest year for which data are available.

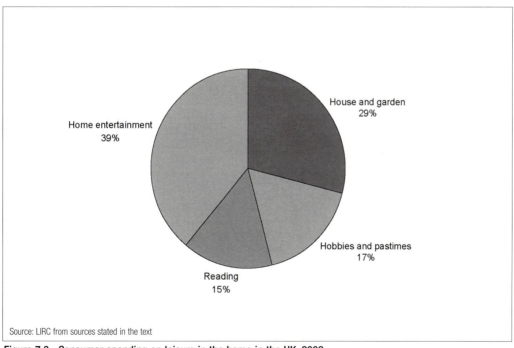

Source: LIRC from sources stated in the text

Figure 7.3   Consumer spending on leisure in the home in the UK, 2002

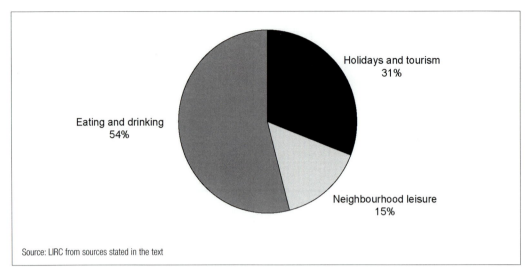

Source: LIRC from sources stated in the text

Figure 7.4 Consumer spending on leisure away from home in the UK, 2002

Review of 2001

The year 2001 was exceptional for leisure spending since we saw the synthesis of two shocks in spending in the UK economy: the foot and mouth epidemic and the effect of the 11th September terrorist attacks. Real consumer spending growth rate peaked in 1999 at 4.3%, but since then decreased to 3.6% in real terms, representing a value of £626.1 billion in 2001. The household saving ratio, defined as household savings divided by household income, decreased sharply, from 10% in 1995 to 5% in 2001. This boosted the long-term trend of leisure growth caused by low levels of interest rates, increases in personal disposal incomes, the extra spending generated by technological innovation and the perceived temporary shocks to the economy.

Since 1999, a 7.9% increase in the volume of consumer spending brought about a 5.1% change in leisure spending. Growth in leisure spending for the year 2001 was lower than previously expected because of the special factors mentioned above.

The growth of consumer spending in leisure was greater in the home sector in 2001. The sectors with the largest growth in 2001 were spirits, television and pets. This compares with toys, holidays overseas and PCs (mainly because of PC games) in 2000. The

growth rate of the volume of holidays overseas dropped from 10.5% in 2000 to 0.2% in 2001, mainly because of the 11th September shock. Overall in 2001, we had 1.1% growth in the volume of consumer spending on leisure with particularly strong growth in hobbies and pastimes (5.5%), alcoholic drink (4.9%) and house and gardening (4.3%) (see Table 7.2). This is the lowest rate of growth since the recession year 1991 when the leisure sector reduced in size by 3.4%. The forces behind the growing sectors are the popularity of city living, digital photography and spirits – especially ready-to-drink spirits – among young people, and the boom in the housing market because of low interest rates. Additionally the foot and mouth disease and 11th September effects have directed resources towards the domestic market, benefiting gardening and DIY in particular.

In 2001 many leisure sectors were in recession. The biggest decline was in sightseeing (down 12.5%). This sector has suffered both from the effects of foot and mouth disease, as internal tourism dropped, and from the after-effects of the 11th September attacks, which reduced foreign tourism, affecting mainly the London market. UK holiday accommodation was mainly a casualty of foot and mouth disease and dropped in volume by 11%. The same is true of gambling (−3.9%), mainly because of the

Table 7.2   Forecasts of key economic indicators, June 2002

Forecasts	By the Treasury (% change)	By independent forecasters (% change)			By LIRC (% change)
		Average	High	Low	
Gross domestic product (GDP) – constant prices					
2002	2.0–2.5	1.9	2.7	0.4	2.0
2003	2.75–3.25	2.8	3.6	-0.1	2.8
Consumer spending – constant price prices					
2002	2.75–3.0	3.1	3.7	1.9	3.4
2003	2.25–2.75	2.5	3.6	0.3	2.4
Retail prices					
2002	2.25	2.2	3.1	1.6	2.3
2003	2.5	2.4	3.3	1.5	2.3
Unemployment (millions)					
2002	n/a	1.06	1.20	0.91	1.03
2003	n/a	1.05	1.35	0.66	1.06

Sources: HM Treasury *Forecasts for the UK Economy*, LIRC

cancellation of many horse racing meetings. Reading declined by 2.8% as result of the crisis that hit the magazine sector and the continuous decline of newspaper circulation. The UK entertainment media sector – including cable and satellite television operators, film companies and magazine publishers – was severely squeezed by cutbacks in corporate advertising budgets. Finally, although holidays overseas have not been in decline, they grew by only 0.2% mainly because of the 11th September events. On average prices in the leisure sector increased by 2.8% in 2001. There has been long-term price deflation in home entertainment – especially video, audio equipment and PCs – holidays overseas, photography, and toys and games. The sectors with the highest rates of inflation are local entertainment (5.8% price inflation in 2001) and holidays in the UK (7.8% price inflation in 2001).

Economic assumptions

In order to forecast the leisure market we need first to specify the assumptions on which the forecast is based and then make an informed judgement by pooling all the available forecasts from other agencies together, as discussed in Chapter 6.

Other forecasts relate mainly to key economic variables that determine leisure expenditures. Table 7.2 shows forecasts for 2002 and 2003 for key economic indicators from the major economic forecasting agencies. The Leisure Industries Research Centre predicted 2% growth in real GDP (at constant prices) in 2002 followed by a further 2.8% growth in 2003. This is at the low end of the Treasury's 2002 forecast. LIRC predicted that consumer spending would grow faster than this in real terms: 3.4% in 2002 and 2.4% in 2003; and expected inflation to remain below the government's 2.5% target at 2.3% in 2002 and 2.3% in 2003.

Short-term forecast

The UK's retail sector recorded their strongest growth in six years during March 2002. According to the British Retail Consortium, like for like sales rose by 7.5% compared with the previous year, the

Table 7.3   Growth in real consumer spending on leisure, 2001–2003

Consumer spending on leisure	Volume of spending (% change)		
	2001	2002	2003
Reading	−2.8	0.3	0.2
Home entertainment	3.6	4.0	6.7
House and garden	4.3	6.2	4.1
Hobbies and pastimes	5.5	4.3	2.6
Leisure in the home	3.3	4.2	4.5
Eating out	0.5	3.5	1.4
Alcoholic drinks	4.9	2.3	1.3
Eating and drinking	2.8	2.9	1.3
Local entertainment	2.2	2.4	0.9
Gambling	−3.9	2.1	1.0
Active sport	0.9	4.8	2.7
Neighbourhood leisure	−0.4	3.5	1.8
Sightseeing	−12.5	19.0	0.9
UK holiday accommodation	−11.0	31.2	−0.2
Holidays overseas	0.2	7.6	5.1
Holidays and tourism	−2.9	10.5	3.7
Leisure away from home	0.3	5.5	2.2
All leisure	1.1	5.2	2.9

Source: *Leisure Forecasts* 2002–2006

biggest rise since 1996. The DIY and gardening sectors recorded the strongest growth as home owners undertook some improvements during the Easter break. Decoration, garden furniture and picnic hampers were especially popular among shoppers. Electronic goods showed a mixed picture, with mobile phones selling poorly while the latest DVD technology and widescreen televisions sold well.

The terrorist attacks on 11th September changed the shape of the economic cycle in the UK. Before the attacks UK economic growth was likely to strengthen in 2002 after a modest slowdown in 2001 in response to lower interest rates. But, with consumer and business confidence globally affected by the attacks, GDP growth was predicted to be 2% in 2002. Nevertheless it implied that the UK would escape recession overall, something that could not be achieved by the US, Japan and Germany. This is re-enforced by very low interest rates, very low inflation, stable oil prices, strong public finances and an expansionary fiscal policy. It is important to emphasise that it is the strength of consumption that was sustaining GDP while the manufacturing sector was in the grip of severe recession. Britain's labour market survived the most severe downturn in the global economy in a decade, with an overall increase in the unemployment claimant count of only 400 people between September 2001 and February 2002. This is the immediate period after the 11th September attacks.

The modest growth in GDP was forecast to be accompanied by a generous growth in consumer spending. This was fuelled partly by falling ratios of savings. This is not a problem in the short term, as a big proportion of savings is directed towards the housing market. The accompanied rise in house prices generated extra wealth but not necessarily extra consumption. Whenever house prices rise, the price of housing services rises in proportion. Unless homeowners can reduce their consumption of housing services, perhaps by trading down to a smaller house, they cannot realise the apparent gain in their home wealth. However, house owners can realise some of their increased wealth by increasing the size of their mortgage and there was some evidence of this taking place in 2002, further fuelling consumption. In the long term, the biggest risk for the economy is that macro-economic policy has been relaxed in the wake of the US terrorist attacks, fuelling the continuation of the UK consumer boom and threatening the eventual re-emergence of inflation. This is similar to the way that policy was loosened excessively following the 1987 stock market crash, leading to the inflationary problems that eventually contributed to the recession. However this is unlikely to happen today.

Effect of the 11th September attacks

The short-term forecast is affected by the 11th September events and the aftermath of the foot and mouth epidemic. The UK tourism sector, already reeling from the foot and mouth crisis, was hit particularly hard in 2001 by a drop in overseas visitors in the wake of 11th September. Hotels, guesthouses and tourist attractions in the UK are estimated to have lost about £2 billion in revenues in 2001. The housing market, which rose strongly over the summer of 2001, cooled following the 11th September attacks. A surge in the number of people buying properties to let is fuelling the house price boom, particularly among smaller properties in London and the south. Paradoxically the terrorist attacks in the US had a stimulating effect for some parts of the UK market. Retailers had the strongest December sales for five years. December 2001 sales were 6% above the previous year's levels, on a like for like basis, and compared favourably to the more anaemic growth of 3.4% recorded in December 2000. The recorded rate was three times the pace of growth of the economy as a whole, and comes at a time when many high profile retailers were suffering from the slump in the number of visitors to the UK. In fact, the rate of growth in consumer spending mapped inversely the rate of decline in holidays abroad. The same growth occurred in November, with total sales up 8.2%, so this was not an isolated end of year phenomenon. It was extremely surprising, especially because 2001 saw a steady deterioration in economic conditions and major falls in share prices. Consumer and business confidence slid. International economic bodies such as the IMF and the OECD revised their economic growth projections for 2001 and 2002 downwards repeatedly because of the weakening economic climate. The media have been dominated by talk of recession for more than half a year, and especially since 11th September.

Many economic observers thought that the recent boom in spending was a result of the very low cost of borrowing in the UK. Indeed between February and November 2001 the Bank of England cut rates by two percentage points in seven steps to a 37-year low of 4%. Others thought that the UK consumers were switching their tastes from outdoor leisure to indoor leisure. Although there is truth in both these arguments it is important to recognise that part of the UK domestic market experienced a totally surprising uplift as direct result of what happened in New York. The most important mechanism was what happened to consumers' travelling budgets. Long holidays abroad were cancelled or postponed. Holiday cancellation usually implies that the holiday funds are spent somewhere else rather than saved. This benefited shorter domestic holidays and domestic forms of leisure spending like DIY, gardening, DVDs, sport clothing and footwear. A survey by the English Tourism Council (October 22, 2001) identified nearly one million people who had decided to take a domestic holiday rather than venture abroad. Another two million decided to wait and see.

Leisure market in 2002

Overall 2002 will see 5.2% growth in the volume of consumer spending on leisure (Figure 7.5). There will be strong growth in away from home leisure, particularly in UK holiday accommodation (31.2%), sightseeing (19%) and holidays overseas (7.6%). These sectors that suffered worst in 2001 will recover and achieve the highest growth. This is the only year of the immediate future where away from home leisure will grow at a higher rate than leisure in the home. Overall, therefore the short-term outlook for 2002 is very optimistic.

Reduced growth rates in 2003

Leisure spending will continue to grow in 2003 but at a slower rate. Two sectors with relatively high rates of growth will be home entertainment (6.7%), driven by an explosion in DVD demand, and holidays overseas (5.1%). Most leisure sectors will show a pattern of reduced growth rates in 2003 compared with 2002. Other short-term constraints on leisure demand include interest rate increases and the continuing reduced level of overseas visitors (particularly for the London area).

Long-term forecast

The demand for leisure is highly cyclical because it mainly depends on real personal disposable income and consumers' discretionary spending. This is illustrated in Figure 7.5, which shows the growth of consumers' expenditure and leisure spending from

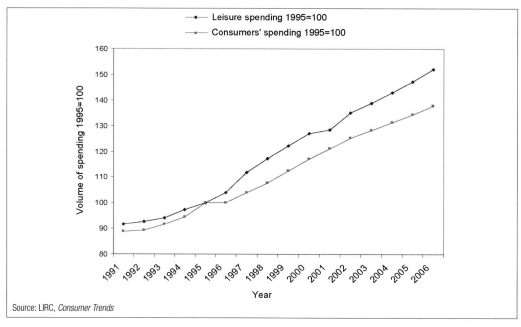

Figure 7.5 Consumer spending and leisure spending, UK, 1991–2006

1991 to 2006. It contrasts the large swing in the first half of the 1990s and the one-off shock in 2001 with the steady growth of leisure spending in late 1990s and the long-term forecast to 2006.

Traditionally, leisure spending grows faster than consumer spending as a whole in boom years but it also grows slower, or declines faster, than overall consumer spending in a recession. Thus we saw sharp cut-backs in leisure spending in the deep recessions of the early 1980s and again in the early 1990s. If the economy swings from boom to recession, the swings in leisure spending will be more severe than the swings in the economy. However, the UK economic cycles have become more muted since 1995. Economic policy is contributing towards muted 'mini cycles'. The result, as Figure 7.5 shows, is that leisure spending has continued to grow at a faster rate than the economy as a whole resulting in an acceleration in the rate at which leisure takes an increasing share of total consumer spending. Thus in 1996 leisure spending accounted for 27.9% of total consumer spending. By 2006 this will rise to 29%, which is a much faster rate of increase than was the case in the 1980s and

early 1990s, as indicated by the widening gap illustrated in Figure 7.5.

Consumer expenditure in the long term will grow by 2.3–2.5%. The associated growth in leisure expenditure in real terms will be 3–3.3%. The housing market will continue growing on average by 6.25% annually, a rate much higher than inflation. Given low levels of interest rates, investment in housing improvements will become an attractive proposition.

Travelling is a factor that increasingly influences the level of expenditure in the rest of the economy. A global market is not characterised only by mobility of capital and labour. Cultural exchange and international tourism is a necessary part. Increasingly people budget for holidays as a matter of course.

A large part of the population takes at least one holiday abroad every year. The World Tourism Organisation estimated a long-term growth rate of 4.1% a year in international tourism for the period up to 2020. This could still be a conservative forecast despite the depressing headlines of September 2002.

In the UK, a population of 59 million recorded almost 57 million visits abroad in the year 2000. This represents an increase of 82% during the last ten years. The size of the holiday budget has increased rapidly in this period. The way the holiday budget is spent influences the state of the leisure market. If domestic mobility (as in the case during the foot and mouth crisis) is restricted, a large part of the leisure market is going to be negatively affected, while the loss of domestic tourism spending is directed towards holidays abroad as well as sectors of home leisure such as gardening, DIY and DVDs.

Stronger growth in home leisure

Figure 7.6 compares the growth rates in volume of spending on home leisure and away leisure between 1999 and 2006. We can distinguish four stages of development. First, in the years 1999 and 2000 the home leisure sector has higher growth rates than the away from home leisure sector. The driving force is technological innovation and substitution of old products for new (for example PCs). Second, in 2001 away from home leisure spending collapsed because of the effect of foot and mouth disease and the 11th September attacks. Away from home leisure

depends crucially on tourism and freedom of movement. It usually expands rapidly (as in 1997), when tourism drove the market. Third, in 2002 we expect the away from home leisure to recover and because it is rebounding from a very low point, its growth rate will exceed the rate of growth of home leisure for the first time since 1998. Fourth, after 2002, home leisure will consistently outperform away leisure, as new technology in television, photography, DVDs and so on generates new expenditure.

Finally it is worth re-emphasising that in spite of its dynamism spending on home leisure is still considerably less in absolute terms than spending on away leisure. The latter accounts for 75% of total leisure spending.

Home leisure sectors

Figure 7.7 shows the forecast rates of growth in the home leisure market from 2001 to 2006. Home leisure spending is expected to grow by 26% overall from 2001 to 2006. The highest growth will occur in the television sector (57% growth over the period), followed by CDs, records and tapes (40%). These two sectors are consistently the highest

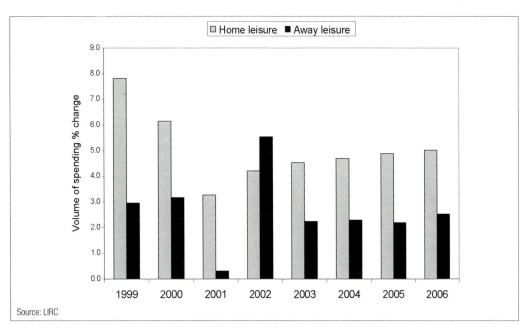

Source: LIRC

Figure 7.6 Growth in home and away leisure markets, 1999–2006

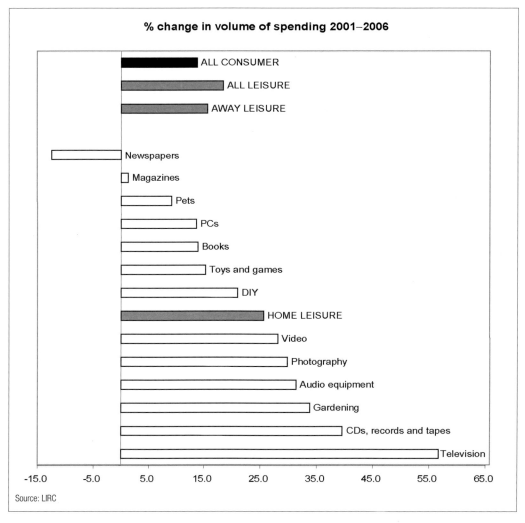

% change in volume of spending 2001–2006

Figure 7.7 Forecast rates of growth in home leisure market, 2001–2006

growth sectors of the home leisure market. Television, in particular, will have a very strong long-term growth because of the digital television revolution. The analogue signal will be switched off in 2010 and the recent setback from the collapse of ITV Digital will not reverse growth. We have revised upwards our expectations for gardening (34% growth) and photography (30% growth). Photography will be boosted in the long run by the substitution of digital cameras for non-digital. Gardening on the other hand is boosted by a change of tastes. A garden will be increasingly viewed as a place for socialising and eating (weather permitting) with more expenditure on garden furniture and barbecues. The magazine sector will grow over the five-year period by only 1%. This reflects the strong competition from the Internet for reading time, and the sudden collapse of the men's magazines sub-sector. Newspapers is the only sector with negative growth. Books is the only sector of printed media that holds its own and continues to flourish even under the new hi-tech environment. The video, photography, audio equipment, gardening, CDs, records and television sectors will perform above the average of the home leisure sector.

Away leisure sectors

Figure 7.8 shows the expected rates of growth in the away leisure market over the period 2001 to 2006. Away leisure spending is expected to grow by 16% overall from 2001 to 2006. The highest growth will occur in the holidays overseas sector (31% growth over the period), followed by holidays in the UK by UK residents. The forecast has been revised substantially from 2001 to incorporate the uncertainty following the 11th September attacks. However, despite that setback, holidays abroad will be encouraged in the 2001 to 2006 period by reduced prices of airfares. In this period no-frills operators such as EasyJet and Ryanair will expand further in the market. The high growth of holidays in the UK in 2002 is partly an 'illusion' reflecting the low point of the sector in 2001. The same is true about sightseeing. The beer sector will have negative growth, but the spirits sector has turned the corner driven by the popularity of ready-to-drink products. We expect that this is not a one-year craze and will have long-term consequences for the industry. Away leisure will benefit from rises in disposable incomes in the long run and the relative strength of sterling in the short run.

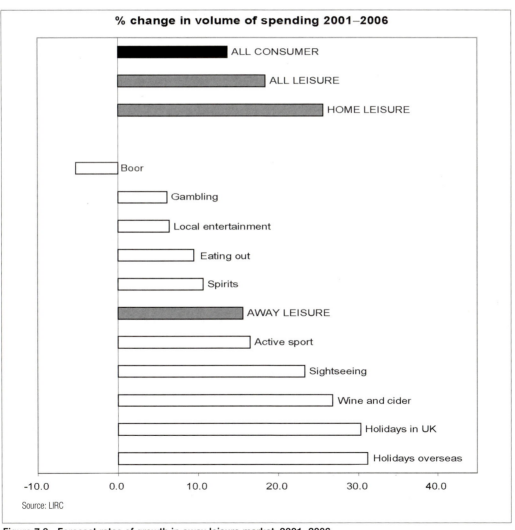

Figure 7.8   Forecast rates of growth in away leisure market, 2001–2006

Lessons from the past, pointers to the future

If in 1975 we had been asked to forecast the major trends in leisure for the last quarter of the 20th century, what would we have got wrong, and what can we learn from such mistakes in making long-term forecasts for the next 25 years?

Forecasting individual markets

If forecasting the major forces that affect leisure markets is difficult, how difficult is it to forecast the leisure market as a whole and individual sectors within it? As the first section of this chapter explains, if we can forecast the growth of consumer expenditure as a whole reasonably well, then we can also forecast the growth of leisure expenditure: in general, leisure expenditure grows slightly faster than consumer expenditure as a whole. This is also true of most individual leisure markets. However, within the leisure sector there will be areas of rapid expansion and other areas of equally rapid decline.

One spectacular example of the rise and fall of the demand for a leisure product is British cinema attendance in the 20th century. From a demand level of virtual zero at the start of the century, cinema grew to be the most popular leisure activity in Britain with peak attendance at 1,635 million in 1946. Since that year, attendance declined dramatically to reach 55 million in 1985. Looking forward 25 years from 1975, one thing would have been easy to forecast: the continued decline in cinema admissions. Yet 1985 proved to be a watershed, and since then cinema attendance has increased every year with the sole exception of 1998. Attendance now stands at close to three times the level of 1985. Forecasting certainties do not exist in the leisure sector. Cinema attendance is not the only area of leisure to show this yo-yo effect. Professional football attendance also rose continually over the post-war period to reach a peak in 1948–9 at 41.25 million. Figure 7.9 shows the steady decline to around 16 million in 1985. This should have been a relatively easy market to forecast in

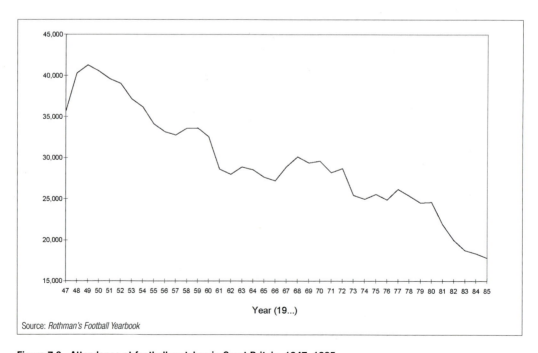

Source: *Rothman's Football Yearbook*

Figure 7.9   Attendance at football matches in Great Britain, 1947–1985

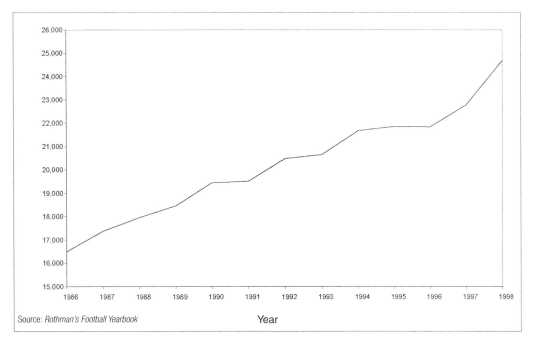

Figure 7.10   Attendance at football matches in Great Britain, 1986–1998

1975, but yet again the long-term decline was reversed from 1986 onwards and Figure 7.10 shows a healthy growing market in the 1990s. There is an inherent volatility in leisure markets that makes it dangerous to forecast long term.

Lessons for the new millennium

In addition to the problems mentioned above, over the next 25 years technology will deliver new ways of using leisure time that nobody can yet imagine. We have only been able to illustrate this by giving examples of leisure products that have been introduced over the last 25 years in the second section of this chapter. The speed with which such new products are being introduced is increasing not diminishing. Also, as the cinema and football spectating examples illustrate, old products will be seen in a new light and generate a new, different type of demand. The football example, in particular, illustrates that consumers may look for more authentic leisure experiences and excitement, just as technology is giving them more and more opportunities for virtual or simulated experiences. There is one thing we can be sure of when making long-term leisure forecasts: we will always be wrong to some extent.

Part III

Supply in sports, leisure and tourism

8 Analysing market structures in leisure and tourism

Dr Brian Davies Division of Economics, Staffordshire University

Focus questions

- Why study market shares?
- What other sources of data are necessary?
- What information is needed?

- How should firms measure market share?
- How can firms use official data to derive estimates of unobserved variables?

Introduction

Tourism is of central importance to most economies and has so expanded as to be seen by many global organisations as 'the world's largest industry'. For example, the World Travel and Tourism Council estimates that travel and tourism will generate $9,285.9 billion annually by 2011, which would constitute 4.2% of world gross domestic product or 12.5% of all exports. One of the important characteristics of tourism is that it is an environment of volatility implying a high level of business risk. Explanations of the causes of volatility concentrate on the market environment and especially demand. Other chapters in this book illustrate this and show that this has led to an emphasis on market segmentation and the formulation of policy to take into account the diverse nature of tourism demand. What is not as well served is an examination of the supply environment. This chapter begins this analysis by outlining the importance of understanding the supply side of the business environment. It then presents the theoretical framework necessary to provide this understanding before examining in detail how one can empirically measure the business environment and in particular industrial concentration to generate an understanding of competition in relevant markets.

The importance of understanding the business environment

The influence of suppliers on each other, while having attracted great attention in the manufacturing sectors of economies, has hardly been examined in services in general and in tourism provision specifically. Yet many aspects need appraising. What is the level of concentration in tourism sectors? Is concentration a good or a bad thing for firms and for the public interest? How do operators conduct themselves? On what basis are prices established? Are the markets competitive or contestable? What are the roles of product differentiation, barriers to entry, collusion and restrictive practices (if they exist), and other such potential influences on the conduct of firms in their relations with each other? An understanding of such issues, together with structural changes undergone in the last 20 years, may inform future policy considerations at governmental and at firm level.

At the governmental level, such an understanding may be important for keeping official records and for shaping policy aimed at encouraging competition. For commercial organisations within the tourism industry, planning, marketing and strategy derived from understanding of market structure and power will be better informed. Further, the two may impinge on each other. Commercial decisions may lead to policy on competition and competition policy may influence a firm's behaviour.

In the tour operator and travel agency sector several investigations have taken place. These include the UK Monopolies and Mergers Commission (MMC) investigation of the Thomson–Horizon merger in 1989, the Office of Fair Trading's investigation of package tours in 1994 and the European Commission's 2000 ruling on Airtours' bid for First Choice.

In order to investigate these issues and understand the MMC (now renamed the Competition Commission) and European Commission's findings, a supply side approach is required. The MMC ruled that the merger could stand on the basis that it would not operate against the public interest. Having considered the effects of the merger on outbound All Inclusive Tours, leisure travel by air, retail travel agents and the implications of vertical integration between such sectors, the Commission concluded that such markets had strong, if changing, growth. Competition was extensive and entry by new firms continued. Hence, it was felt that competition would not be sufficiently diminished by the merger so as adversely to affect prices, choice or standard of customer service.

The Airtours bid was rejected on the grounds of oligopoly 'collective dominance' among the three largest undertakings – Thomson, Thomas Cook and the enlarged Airtours – which would remain in the market. The Commission suggested this would limit the supply of charter airline seats and travel agency services to smaller, non-integrated operators thus impeding competition. The four principal operators giving preference to their own products would create high barriers to entry. Smaller, independent tour operators' ability to compete is dependent on the availability of such airline charter seats and travel agency services. Removing First Choice as a source of supply of airline seats and travel agency services would increase the incentive for large operators to restrict capacity strengthening their position to implement strategies designed to limit competition.

Both investigations undertook an examination of the nature of producer competition and industrial performance between firms in the tourism business. Such supply side activity is often evaluated in terms of the degree of industry concentration as being indicative of barriers to entry and the restriction of competition. The theoretical basis of such investigations rests on the structure–conduct– performance (SCP) and industrial organisation (IO) paradigms. Indeed, this is reflected in the construction, historically, of business statistics.

The structure–conduct–performance and industrial organisation paradigms

The SCP paradigm encapsulates the following propositions about the nature of industrial concentration:

*   The structure of markets determines a firm's behaviour and performance.
*   Under imperfect competition, firms may earn persistent profits and produce at an inefficient level of output.

However, the SCP approach has its critics and has led to the development of the IO paradigm. This paradigm embraces several alternative hypotheses to the idea that market structure determines firm behaviour and performance. According to the IO paradigm persistent profits may be the result of:

*   strategic games among firms
*   the internal organisational efficiency in firms
*   the need for firms to be efficient to meet any potential, as opposed to actual, threats of entry by new players.

The IO approach embraces the following general propositions:

*   Profitability is positively related to market characteristics proxying market power and/or efficiency.
*   The absence of such a relationship conversely implies the existence of real competition or the market is contestable as the result of potential competition.

The empirical analysis of competition

The above general proposition suggests that any market power investigation of firm and industrial behaviour will require information concerning the classification of businesses and data allowing the construction of market shares and concentration variables. The following section outlines and discusses various steps that would be useful in this endeavour.

Step 1: Using business classifications

In the UK, the official business classification system derives from the Standard Industrial Classification of Economic Activities (SIC). SIC was first constructed in 1948 as a method of classifying business establishments (and others) by type of economic activity they are engaged in. It uses a hierarchical digit system with which industries can be classified according to different levels of aggregation. Thus, 'a common framework of classification is provided leading to consistent data collection, tabulation, presentation and analysis' (ONS); see Chapter 2. It is clear that ideas associated with the SCP approach underpinned the 1948 statistics. Moreover, manufacturing dominated the data, consistent with the engines of growth in the UK at the time.

The methodology used by the UK Office for National Statistics follows international standards. The Nomenclature generale des Activités economiques dans les Communautés Européennes (NACE) regulation placed an obligation on the UK to produce a new Standard Industrial Classification guaranteeing national and Community classifications and statistics comparability. The revision of SICs began in 1980 and then continued in 1990 when European Community regulations revised NACE. From 1992, SICs conform to EU NACE Rev 1. The 2003 UK SIC conforms to NACE Rev 1:1. This constitutes a minor revision of the European Community classification system and is a response to UK user demand for more details at the 5-digit subclass level.

Principal industrial activity is taken as the basis of classification. Here, principal activity is defined as the activity, which contributes most to the gross value added at factor cost of the unit being surveyed. It should be noted that principal activity does not necessarily account for 50% or more of the total value added. Where information on value added is not available other criteria are used – gross output, value of sales, wages and salaries, and employment. However, the broad change to principal activity illustrates recognition of the need to modify the basis of calculating the statistics from the historical emphasis on manufacturing. Originally, SICs were not over concerned with certain activities –

especially tourism – and had great emphasis on primary and secondary production, for example chemical and manufacturing. This was not so much the SIC misguidedly over-concentrating on manufacturing in the early days, but rather other parts of the actual economy such as services were relatively less important then. However, several revisions have taken place to reflect the changing economic reality. New products, new industries and changes in emphasis for existing industries have been accommodated. The last major update occurred in 1992. In tourism areas, for example, the former (1980) division of hotels and catering became hotels and restaurants while transport and communications together with tourist offices, radio and television transmission have become a section known as transport, storage and communications. (Some reclassification occurred in 2003, which is examined later.) The principal activity is then further classified by a six-stage 'top-down' method of attaching digits as illustrated in Box 8.1.

Box 8.1

Assigning SIC digits to classify activity

Stage 1: List the activities carried out by the unit and calculate the value added by each

Stage 2: Identify the section; assign single-digit code

Stage 3: Identify the division; assign double-digit code

Stage 4: Identify the group; assign triple-digit code

Stage 5: Identify the class; assign four-digit code

Stage 6: Identify the subclass assign five-digit code

Source: ONS UK SIC 1992 *Methodological Guide*

NACE REV 1 has four digit classes but, as illustrated in Box 8.1, SICs have been extended to a five-digit system to facilitate subclasses. As noted above, the digit system is hierarchical from the highest level of aggregation down to the fifth digit subclasses, although not all digits are used in each class. For example, air transport is divided into the following five digit classes:

62.10/1 Scheduled passenger air transport

62.10/2 Other scheduled air transport

62.20/1 Non-scheduled passenger air transport

62.20/2 Other non-scheduled air transport

There have been mild criticisms of such tourism codes. However, it must be borne in mind how classifications are determined. The first 4 levels down to and including the Class level, are decided at a European level. The UK is only one voice in the work that develops each generation of the EU industrial activity classification system.

Other relevant SICs for tourism include:

55 Hotels; restaurants (5530)

63 Activities of travel agents and tour operators; tourist assistance activities not elsewhere classified

60 Land transport; transport via pipelines including (6010) Transport via railway and (6120) Inland water transport

62 Air transport including (6210) Scheduled air transport and (6220) Non-scheduled air transport

Once the classes are established, industry level data are to be found in the Annual Business Inquiry published by the UK government to replace both the Census of Production and Business Monitors. Of particular relevance is the Distribution and Services section including, for example, Section H – Hotels and Restaurants.

Data are given for:
- number of enterprises
- total turnover
- approximate gross value added at basic prices
- total purchases of goods, materials and services
- total employment point in time
- total employment average during the year
- total employment costs

- total net capital expenditure
- total net capital expenditure – acquisitions
- total net capital expenditure – disposals
- total stocks and work in progress – value at end of year
- total stocks and work in progress – value at beginning of year
- total stocks and work in progress – increase during the year

It is also possible to obtain quarterly turnover data on service trades from the quarterly Distribution and Services Trades release, although the range of data is more limited than the Annual Business Inquiry.

Annual Business Inquiry data can be accessed at National Statistics Online, at www.statistics.gov.uk/abi. The Distribution and Services Trades news release can be found under Latest Releases on the same website.

This information could be useful for aggregate and time series analysis. More detailed firm specific analysis, however, requires firm-level data and the construction of market share and concentration variables.

Step 2: Identifying firm-level data and the construction of market shares and concentration variables

As discussed earlier, under the SCP approach, market structure is considered to be the important determinant of the degree of competition in an economic activity. Two significant influences on structure are considered to be the degree of industry concentration and the extent of barriers to entry. There are two general propositions relating to industrial concentration:

- Concentration refers to the distribution of market shares according to the number of firms in the activity.
- The higher the percentages of supply by the lower the number of firms, the higher the concentration and the lower the levels of competition.

In line with the general propositions of the IO paradigm, the neo-classical economics view is that high concentration means low competition allowing firms to be inefficient and to exercise market power to the detriment of their customers and the economy in general. In early manufacturing studies there was a propensity to measure the degree of concentration in terms of a seller concentration ratio. A concentration ratio (CR) calculates the percentage share of a market supplied by a specified number of firms and can be based on sales, employment, assets or value added. Thus a six-firm concentration ratio might measure the proportion of, for example, total output produced by the six largest firms in an industrial sector and is usually represented in a form such as 6CR = 60%. This indicates that the top six firms have a market share of 60% with the remaining 40% being accounted for by the rest of the industry. The Department of Industry, using data from the Census of Production classified according to SICs, published such ratios until the mid-1980s in Business Monitors. However, for many tourism activities in the UK no concentration ratios were available. Nevertheless, these could be calculated by taking the value of sales of the largest firms, say, 6 in a 6CR, divided by the total market sales of the defined industry.

The second influence is that of barriers to entry. The existence and degree of barriers to entry may indicate:

- the ease or otherwise of entry for new firms
- the degree of security existing firms may have from new competition entering.

Thus:

High barriers = low entry
Low barriers = high entry

It is argued in the SCP literature that the existence of concentration will be directly linked to barriers to entry. Such barriers create entry costs that the incumbents do not have to face. The lag of entry is important – the longer the time scale, the less likelihood of entry. Clearly, in tourism, the lag for travel agencies is short given that the capital required to set up an agency does not have to be expensive and business can be opened almost within days. For establishing airline companies and some types of attractions the lag of entry will be longer. Substantial investment and capital raising is required with long pay-back periods. Suggested barriers are economies of scale, absolute cost advantage, product differentiation and capital requirements. In principle these could be calculated from firm data on expenditures. These are not readily available, however. The remainder of the chapter focuses on making use of the firm-level data that are available.

Steps 3–5: Using firm and data information

As implied above, in order to construct meaningful variables to make use of IO analysis, both industry size and firm-level information are required together with appropriate data. Variables to represent market share and concentration require annual data on turnover and pre-tax profits, both for the total industry being considered and at the firm level. The market share variable is constructed by taking the share of each firm's turnover to total industry turnover. The concentration variable, as noted above, may take the form of a seller concentration ratio.

Industry level data can be derived from the SIC-based Annual Business Inquiry, as noted above, whereas at the firm level, official data are found wanting. The gap has to be filled from alternative, reliable sources. In the case of tourism, important data are available in commercially produced information. An important source is micro data based on financial information that companies are legally obliged to place in the public domain. Here, commercially produced data are available including One Source and Financial Analysis Made Easy (FAME). One Source publishes data for up to ten years for over 100,000 private and public companies with a turnover in excess of £500,000 per annum. The data are derived from the ICC Information Group's British Companies Database. FAME is published by Dijk Electronic Publishing and consists of listings of 1.8 million UK and Irish public and private companies. 500,000 of these are in detailed format with up to ten years' information.

However, there are still difficulties because commercial sources such as FAME classify activities according to SICs; this makes it difficult to find certain categories because of the relatively poor coverage of tourism. Where SICs exist, as in hotels and restaurants, it is necessary to locate the SIC and obtain totals, such as turnover, for the whole sector as defined by the government. The required data at the firm level have to be obtained from the commercial source. To do this, it is necessary to have the name of at least one firm in the sector. On the plus side, FAME gives you access to all the peer firms in that category.

Step 6: Discussing caveats: problems of definition

As well as the ingenuity required to obtain data for analysis, there are important conceptual caveats that should be noted in employing the IO approach. While some of these caveats are general they are particularly acute in relation to tourism activity.

Is tourism production similar to manufacturing?

Conventional SCP economics, which as implied earlier provided an important rationale underpinning official business data collection, views the firm as a black box of technological and managerial relationships. Inputs are turned into outputs that are often technically identical and the boundaries of the firm are given. The result is a particular standardised process. Viewing the production of a tourism commodity in the same way is questionable. The tourism product can be considered to be heterogeneous consisting of a complex bundle of characteristics based round, but often incidental to, the motivations of tourists. As a consequence, the nature of inputs tends to be more eclectic and from a greater diversity of sources than in manufacturing. Although tangible inputs are necessary in both sectors, in tourism a vital component involves intangibles. For example, public goods are often part of the product – not just a beach or a natural feature, but also the view.

Outputs may also be less specifically identified than in manufacturing. Again, in tourism the nature of the product is not just the airline seat or hotel bed, but also the experience both before – in deciding where to go and to book – and post consumption – memories and sharing the experiences. Even hotels are more than the consumption of bed space. They are part of the product mix, which includes the experience encountered. At the extreme end, a hotel can be a tourist attraction in its own right as is the Savoy in London. Value added in tourism, therefore,

is more a process of combining commodified products than one of production that transforms inputs into outputs of a different form. Hence, a physical production function would not be fully representative of the tourism product.

Is tourism an industry?

Tourism may be viewed in several ways. One could argue that it is not one industry but consists of several, connected by a common, but not exclusive, interest in supplying tourists. An alternative view would consider it as an industry because it is composed of firms that jointly co-ordinate goods and services from different industries to meet tourists' needs. Such would be the case in the tour operating industry. Tour operators co-ordinate the activities of several firms in the provision of travel, accommodation and tourist activities. Products will be the result of contracts with third-party suppliers. Firm and industry boundaries are not as clearly defined among tourism suppliers as manufacturers. This may not be as problematic if the aim is to investigate market power and market share within well-defined sectors, say, hotels and restaurants or airlines. However, it may well be with more specifically 'packaged' supply, as in the case of All Inclusive Tours.

There have been some improvements in the SIC classification since 1992, but there is room for more:

- Clearer categorisation is required. For example, British Airways Holidays appears under SIC 6210 scheduled air transport whereas FAME defines this company as a tour operator.
- SIC 6330 is defined as the activities of travel agents and tour operators; tourist assistance activities are not classified elsewhere.
- No SIC exists for the important activity of tourist attractions. For example, Tussauds is classified under SIC 9305 – 'Other service activities not elsewhere classified'. It is interesting to note that before 1992 the equivalent SIC was libraries, museums, art galleries, and so on, indicating that there has been a regressive step in the classification of this category.

While the SICs take main line of business as the basis of categorisation, most 'tourism' companies have other sources of profit from related lines of business. Profits and turnover figures, therefore, contain earnings from other economic activity associated with and/or even outside tourism. Unless the operating units specifically in tourism can be identified, caution needs to be exercised with data and any subsequent findings.

Concentration ratios

As noted above concentration ratios provide a linchpin in IO analysis. Yet, concentration ratios like the 6CR also exhibit interpretative limitations. Important ones are illustrated below.

Different markets may have different structures but produce the same CRs. This suggests that the levels of competition may differ. For example, take the case where 6CR = 60% is found for two markets. Both suggest that the top six companies possess 60% of, say, sales yet the market structures may be different as shown in Table 8.1.

In Market 1 firm A faces less competition than firm A in Market 2. Market 1 has a structure where there is a dominant firm whereas in Market 2 all six large firms have equal shares. The use of an alternative measure of concentration, such as the Herfindahl Index discussed later, may mitigate this problem by including all firms in an industry and giving greater weight to the largest.

Concentration ratios may change over time but do not necessarily reflect changes in competition. For example, a 6CR may rise from 65% to 75% in the next year. However, it may also be possible that the shares of these top six have altered such that the industry is more competitive. Further scenarios are possible. The market may, for example, be contestable rather than competitive. This illustrates that there is a difficulty of interpreting behaviour by merely observing market structure – a feature emphasised by the IO paradigm.

Following on from the problems of definitions, the actual size of the market may be difficult to establish. Should the regional market be taken or the national or the international? Figure 8.1 illustrates conceptually the issues at stake by presenting a set of broadly concentric markets radiating from a domestic core.

Table 8.1 Comparing concentration ratios between two markets

	Market 1		Market 2
	Market share (%)		Market share (%)
Firm A	40	Firm A	10
Firm B	4	Firm B	10
Firm C	4	Firm C	10
Firm D	4	Firm D	10
Firm E	4	Firm E	10
Firm F	4	Firm F	10

Given the nature of the tourism product and the oft-quoted worldwide nature of the activity, this becomes highly important. Should the competition for, say, British Airways be considered against other UK-based carriers or should it be judged against other international carriers like KLM? It could be possible that four firms dominate a regional market with an 80% share, but if it really is a national market the share may be 50%. If it is an international one, then that share may well be below 10%.

On the other hand, low concentration in an international market may disguise high local

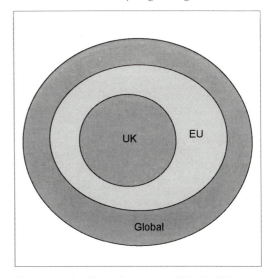

Figure 8.1 The UK tourist market within the EU and global tourist markets

concentration. This may be the case with the tourist attractions market or coach tour operators.

If an industry is defined as the same, or close to, a market then industrial concentration and market concentration become the same thing. If they don't, high industrial concentration may not necessarily mean low competition. While in the IO model the market and the industry are assumed to be both identical and well defined, this may not always be the case. Yet, given the nature of the tourism product drawing from several industries – airlines, hotels, tourist attractions, and so on – the distinction between market and industry is very important. Clearly, the industry definitions contained in SICs create a problem in tourism.

Further, concentration ratios such as 6CR, as illustrated above, discard much useful information for they are only addressing the shares of the few largest firms in an industry. It may be more useful to know about relative sizes of firms and the distribution of firm size throughout an entire industry. A particularly interesting case is that of tour operators and travel agents. This sector of tourism is dominated by vertical integration such that the leading four firms account for about 70% of the market. There then follows a long tail of far in excess of 8,000 companies, from PLCs to owner-managed agencies. How can this sort of characteristic be measured?

As noted above, an alternative measure to simple concentration ratios is the Herfindahl Index. This index facilitates the examination of market shares of *all* firms in a market, not just the largest. The index is calculated using the sum of squares of the market shares of firms in the industry, such that

$$H_j = \Sigma \, S_{ij}^2$$

Where:

  H = Herfindahl Index
  S = Market share of a firm
  Subscript j = market
  Subscript ij = ith firm in market j

Hence 'H' the Herfindahl Index for the jth industry is by definition the sum of squared market shares of all member firms. Values of the index theoretically range from 0 to 1. The value 0 would indicate the theoretical case of perfect competition in which there was an infinite number of very small firms in the market and there was no market power. In contrast, in a monopoly where a single firm is the sole supplier, then the Herfindahl Index will be 1. Lying between these bounds is reality. In these cases, the best way to interpret the index, and to compare industries, is by considering how many firms of equal size could supply the market. For example, an index of 0.2 would indicate that five firms of equal size could supply the market, whereas an index of 0.5 that two firms of equal size could supply the market. The latter case is clearly less competitive in terms of traditional SCP ideas.

A procedure for examining market shares and competition

Taking all these caveats into account, given the data that are presently available, a procedure for examining market share and competition in the tourism industry can be carried out, as illustrated in Figure 8.2.

An example

Let's say we wanted to investigate market shares and competition among UK hotels. The first stage is to determine the SIC. This is listed under the SIC Group Class H: 'Hotels and restaurants'. There then follow a number of sub-categories with further digits. For Hotels the classification takes on a 4-digit number 55.10 Hotels and Motels. Further subdivisions are then made yielding the following:

55.10/1 Hotels and motels with restaurant (licensed)
55.10/2 Hotels and motels with restaurant (unlicensed)
55.10/3 Hotels and motels, without restaurant

The second step involves looking up the Annual Business Inquiry to ascertain the industry level data of total turnover. However, as discussed below, it may be necessary to refine the size of the industry as the Annual Business Inquiry lists Hotels and Restaurants and the subdivisions listed above. Turnover figures are also given for over 120,000 hotels and restaurants. If looking solely at hotels this reduces to still over 10,000. Also the Business Monitor includes several categories of

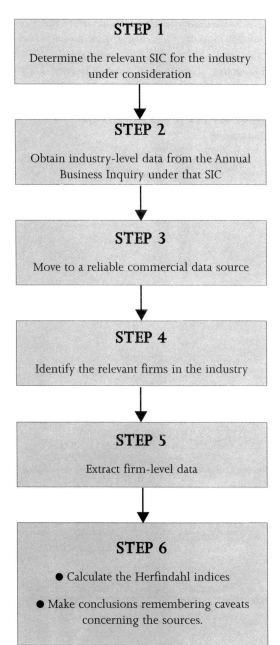

Figure 8.2 Examining competition in the tourism industry

accommodation together with items that may not be considered to be of use in an investigation of hotels. This is an important issue to deliberate, as this figure will form the basis for calculating the Herfindahl

Index. Remembering that market share is based on the share of each hotel firm's turnover of total industry turnover; this needs to be squared and then summed to derive the level of concentration.

It should be emphasised that official data do not reveal individual market shares. In practice it will be necessary to move to a commercial source of data and use the official data as a guide to how representative your analysis is. The commercial source used here, as previously mentioned, is FAME. You will need to go to the Bureau vanDijk Electronic Publishing website on the Internet at www.bvdep.com and register. Once this is complete you can then move to FAME. In the search box type 'hotels' and a list of over 2,600 firms will appear. From the list, you can detect the relevant companies for your investigation by the Primary SIC Code column. Clicking on each firm name will yield an array of statistical information including figures for turnover. These will have to be written down manually for the year you require, or the specific years if you are conducting a time series investigation. The use of a spreadsheet will prove advantageous. Once the firm-level data have been acquired the Herfindahl Index can then be calculated. It is necessary to divide each individual turnover by the total industry turnover to yield each company's individual market share. These are then squared and summated to give the measure of concentration.

Several value judgements will have to be made as the FAME data source only includes firms which are legally required to reveal such information under UK companies' legislation. Over 2,600 firms are listed under 'Hotels'. Clearly this would be an onerous, if not impossible, task to collect all cases and calculate individual company market shares. Further, you may wish to place a limitation on the definitions of the industry in the sense that firms with low turnover may have a weighting not commensurate with their economic importance. It is essential to determine early what the purpose of the research is and, if necessary, to consider which types of hotels are relevant for analysis. In 1999 Davies defined the industry as those firms with an average turnover of around £2 million per annum from 1989 to 1994.

This gave an industry consisting of 36 firms. The individual turnovers of these companies were squared and summed to give the total industry, so defined, turnover for the calculation. The resultant Herfindahl Index calculated had a mean value of 0.151 over the period indicating that this is consistent with an industry dominated by six to seven leading firms. For example, these seven accounted for 62% of total turnover in 1993. The Herfindahl Index suggested that the UK hotel industry was not dissimilar to many manufacturing industries consisting of a small number of large firms and a large number of medium and small firms. It follows that a thorough analysis of competition in such an industry would involve investigating the interaction between such sets of firms. Downward and Davies (2001) have begun to work towards this objective.

Conclusion

This chapter has illustrated a method for examining the fundamental issues concerning market shares and competition, based on a combination of official and commercial data. Clearly, considerable progress has been made in official government statistics since the 1980s in terms of defining the parts of the tourism industry. However, some anomalies remain and it seems worthwhile, in closing, to comment on what further work could usefully be undertaken. The whole study of the supply side of the tourism business would be enhanced by further refinement of SICs together with the inclusion of activities not presently considered. Even the Office for National Statistics recognised limitations when publishing the UK Service Sector Monitor in 2000:

> [UK Service Sector] covers wholesale and retail trades; hotels and restaurants, transport and communications, finance industries, real estate and business activities as well as professional and scientific services. However, not all individual industries are yet covered by the data in this publication.

At least the changes made in relation to SIC 1992 and 2003 together with current work, known as 'Operation 2007', on a major revision to the EU system have gone some way to addressing the needs of the tourism industry. The resultant improved industry-level data should lead to commercially produced firm-level data becoming better defined and refined.

9 Segmenting markets for leisure and tourism

Professor Les Lumsdon Lancashire Business School, University of Central Lancashire
Professor R Elwyn Owen Welsh School of Hospitality, Tourism and Leisure Management, University of Wales Institute, Cardiff

Focus questions

- Why do companies and organisations segment markets in leisure and tourism?
- What are the limitations of segmentation?

- How can segments be measured?
- How are the concepts of segmentation, targeting and positioning related?

Introduction

Expressed in simple terms, market segmentation is the process of classifying buyers of a product or service into discrete groups. As in the business world generally, it has been widely adopted by institutions and businesses operating in the tourism and leisure sector and market segmentation is now a key weapon in their marketing armoury. In this chapter the main reasons for adopting a segmentation approach are outlined, market segmentation is carefully defined and an example of how segmentation works in practice in tourism is offered.

Why market segmentation?

Tourism is a highly competitive activity, and destinations and individual operators are now very much aware of the need to tailor their product or offering and their marketing to the requirements of increasingly experienced, discerning and price conscious consumers. Most tourism businesses have neither the broad product appeal nor the marketing resources to market to an entire population, and they know from experience that a scatter-gun approach will be not be productive. They now realise that it is far more effective to concentrate their efforts on those consumers who, on the basis of past experience and research, appear to be the most likely to buy their product or service offering.

Similarly, destination marketing organisations attach an important role to market segmentation in underpinning their efforts to secure the optimum economic benefit for their area, in the most cost-effective manner. The Wales Tourist Board adopts this approach for the following reasons (WTB, 2000):

- Attempting to communicate with all potential customers will not result in a productive use of limited resources.
- Some groups or segments will generate more business for Wales and deserve to be communicated with more regularly.
- Communications target segments can be tailored, personalised and made to work more effectively.
- Tourism products and services in Wales can be communicated to match the needs of specific segments.

Market segmentation rarely involves concentrating on just one group of consumers and the number of segments identified in practice can vary significantly from one situation to another. Individual leisure businesses rarely put all their eggs in one basket by relying on a single and narrowly defined group of customers in order to succeed; they seek to identify two or more segments with complementary characteristics and product needs. At the micro level, city-based hotels, for example, may focus on the business market during the week and the leisure market at weekends. At the macro level, tourist destinations such as resorts, regions or countries naturally offer a wide variety of tourism products, appealing to wholly different types of consumer, and so they will naturally wish to adopt a more complex market segmentation regime.

Defining market segmentation

The theoretical underpinning of segmentation is well established, especially in relation to visitor profiling and destination choice (Bowen, 1998). Previous research has, for the most part, involved an investigation of segmentation based on a wide range of predefined characteristics of visitors, the most important of which are geo-demographic, socio-economic, psychographic or behavioural descriptors (Kara and Kaynak, 1997). Thus each segment comprises customers who exhibit similar characteristics, motivations or attitudes – they are homogenous in one or more key dimensions. This applies not only to the consumer market. In the business to business market a form of organisational segmentation is also often applied, for example, using criteria such as level or frequency of purchase or volume of order.

In terms of a definition, segmentation refers to the way in which companies and organisations identify and categorise customers into clearly defined groups that possess similar characteristics, needs and desires (McDonald and Dunbar, 1995). The principles of segmentation are based on the premise, first, that a market can be divided into segments for the commercial purpose of targeting customers. Second, it relates to the positioning of the leisure or tourism product or service offering within the market. Many authors use the term product, service or offer interchangeably when referring to tourism. The reader should be aware of this to avoid possible confusion. The term 'product' is often discussed within the context of manufactured or fast moving consumer goods and refers to tangible items such as a kettle or chair. However, the concept has also been extended to include anything that is offered to the market such as people, places and organisations. The term 'offering' or 'service offering' has been used in the service sector in recent years in order to differentiate and explain the composite nature of what is offered to a visitor. In this respect the offer is essentially intangible and the benefits are invariably experiential. For a more detailed discussion see Lumsdon (1997).

The core principles of segmentation

The tourism market, like many other sectors, has been subdivided using a wide range of segmentation techniques, many of which have provided the basis for strategic development of visitor attractions, accommodation provision and destination planning. Segmentation is therefore the first necessary step. The second step relates to the way in which a company then assesses the attractiveness of each segment, which can then be subsequently targeted. The third step involves positioning and this refers to the expectations of a company's customers, or potential customers, in relation to its competitors.

Thus, assuming that a particular market can be readily divided into segments, for the purpose of targeting leisure or tourism offerings it is possible to identify five key underlying principles, which are closely inter-related. A segment has to:

- Be identifiable – It must comprise people who share similar characteristics and/or seek similar benefits from a tourism offering; this is crucial in terms of targeting and positioning of a destination or leisure service. For example, the term 'culture vulture' refers to those who are motivated by visiting a destination to enjoy cultural dimensions.
- Be cohesive – It must be clearly delineated from other segments for measurement purposes – be discrete as well as identifiable. For example, residents who use a leisure centre several times a week are likely to differ significantly in terms of their profile, characteristics and behaviour from those who do so on average just once a month. Frequency of use is the defining factor, which distinguishes the 'dedicated' user from the more casual or incidental user who may attend once a month or less frequently.
- Be measurable – The marketer should be able to estimate the size and value of each market segment. This is important in order to be able to determine whether a segment is viable in a commercial sense. A segment needs to be sufficiently large and/or productive to yield significant use or visitation and revenue. This measurement affords an opportunity to determine

the order of marketing resources that will need to deployed in order to attract customers.

- Be accessible and actionable – An identified segment has to be accessible. Unless a segment can be reached effectively it is not possible to target or position a product or service offering without incurring substantial costs. There needs to be a match between resource level, commitment and achievability in terms of penetrating the defined market segment(s).
- Be substantial – Segments have to be sufficiently large, or if small have a high attributable value, to be pursued for commercial gain or for social marketing purposes.

Methods of segmentation

Smith (1995) argues that there are effectively two broad approaches to segmentation analysis:

- segmentation by trip descriptors, for example, short haul, long haul, visiting friends and relatives (VFR)
- segmentation by tourist descriptors such as 'greys' (early retired and interested in travel) or 'adventurer-explorers' (those seeking unusual and new destinations) or activity seekers.

This is often a useful first stage of analysis where government statistics can be of considerable use. For example, a destination might undertake a segmentation analysis of overseas visitors by trip descriptors. Analysis of data collected as part of the International Passenger Survey (IPS) would enable the researcher to make a preliminary estimate of visitors by originating region and purpose of visit.

Table 9.1 indicates that the largest segment, in terms of volume, is the business market, which accounted for 34% of the total inbound market in 2002. This segment has decreased since 2000. Therefore, tourism authorities might consider it more effective to invest, for example, in a campaign that targets business segments.

Within this general framework, the main factors that have been used to segment tourism markets are benefit segmentation, demographic segmentation, geographic segmentation, psychographic segmentation, buyer behaviour segmentation, personality, multivariate segmentation and organisational segmentation. These are discussed below.

Benefit segmentation

Visitors seek different benefits from a holiday. Some prefer more education than entertainment, some are status seekers and others seek adventure and challenge. Depending on the benefits sought, visitors are likely to place emphasis on different aspects of provision. The evaluation of the level of importance

Table 9.1   Number of visitors to the UK by overseas residents from EU Europe by purposes of visit (all modes), 2000–2002

	2000 (thousands)	2001 (thousands)	2002 (thousands)
Total holiday	4,625	3,765	3,979
Of which inclusive tour	1,315	1,060	956
Business	4,754	4,486	4,735
VFR	3,223	3,267	3,494
Miscellaneous	1,418	1,347	1,579
All visits	14,020	12,865	13,787

Source: ONS (2003) *MQ6 Transport, Travel and Tourism, Overseas Travel and Tourism*

of such attributes is often undertaken; customers weight different features of a service, which are subsequently evaluated to form the basis of benefits analysis. This form of analysis usually requires empirical data to be collected specifically for this purpose.

Demographic segmentation

Primary variables such as age, gender, family life cycle and ethnicity are used to segment markets in tourism. For example, an organisation might be interested in undertaking a segmentation analysis of the UK outbound market by age or gender.

Geographic segmentation

The division of markets according to geographical boundaries is a common form of segmentation in tourism. A tourism provider might segment its domestic market into a number of territorial regions, each with a different propensity to generate customers. It might also do the same for the inbound market. For example, use of the IPS allows analysis of travel by originating regions across the world. In the example shown in Table 9.2 the focus is on visitors to North America from the UK, which highlights the stability of the VFR market in relation to the overall decline in the business and holiday segments between 2000 and 2002.

An extension of this approach makes geodemographic segmentation possible. This approach classifies potential market segments according to the residential neighbourhoods in which they live. One UK application is the ACORN system. The acronym stands for A Classification of Residential Neighbourhoods. Developed by the CACI Market Analysis Group it provides segmentation analysis according to 40 variables combined from data from the population census and other commercial market intelligence. This means that small clusters of housing can be identified as representing particular types of customers, for example, those enjoying high incomes with a propensity to choose adventure holidays.

Psychographic segmentation

Many markets have been segmented according to general lifestyle profiles that include socio-economic characteristics or personality profiles. It is not exactly the same as geodemographics because people within the same neighbourhood might have similar levels of income and aspirations but completely different approaches to lifestyle. Thus, within the market for leisure, the annual publication *Social Trends* provides an analysis of use of time in the household, leisure activities undertaken, participation in pastimes and sports, and so on. It does not, however, allow for segmentation using different key variables.

Buyer behaviour segmentation

Another approach is to segment the market according to type of buying behaviour exhibited by different groups of people. The level of commitment and degree of purchase by groups in relation to a destination or attraction is often considered to be a main starting point of segmentation. For example,

Table 9.2 Number of visitors by air to North America by UK residents by purposes of visit, 2000–2002

	2000 (thousands)	2001 (thousands)	2002 (thousands)
Total holiday	3,051	2,779	2,518
Of which inclusive tour	1,131	1,018	830
Business	963	833	722
VFR	922	947	922
Miscellaneous	120	97	108
All visits	5,056	4,655	4,271

Source: ONS (2003) *MQ6 Transport, Travel and Tourism, Overseas Travel and Tourism*

this approach categorises users according to the level of repeat visits (brand loyalty), or the propensity to use and intensity of use. Empirical data are usually collected for this task. Sometimes a market is segmented according to the values and perceptions held by the visitor that affect the things that they do or wish to do in their leisure time, the type of destination they prefer, and so on. This assumes that people have different attitudes about types of holidays or tourism offerings that are available. Plog (1974), for example, refers to the adventuresome nature of allocentrics, i.e. those who seek out destinations that are unspoilt and characterised by lack of tourism infrastructure.

Box 9.1 provides a practical example of a market segmentation exercise based on consumer behaviour.

It is taken from a study commissioned by the Wales Tourist Board and other partner organisations to develop a cycle tourism strategy for the emerging niche market of cycle tourism. The study concluded that the most appropriate way to segment the cycling market is on the basis of the frequency with which people go leisure cycling, insofar as this determines the types of cycling activity in which people engage, the distances they will cycle and the cycle tourism services they require. The segmentation analysis was based on a variety of sources including previously published data, a qualitative study of existing cycle tourists, a qualitative survey of providers and a quantitative survey of visitors who had previously requested information on cycling.

Box 9.1

Segmentation in cycle tourism

The key cycling tourist market segments are as follows.

Infrequent leisure cyclists:

• people who rarely cycle – they are likely to have cycled as children, but have lapsed as cyclists in adulthood
• people who may own a bike but, if they do, the likelihood is that they hardly ever use it.

Occasional leisure cyclists:

• people who cycle for pleasure a few times during the summer and are unlikely to cycle during the winter; they will usually be bike owners and their primary motivation for going cycling is to discover and enjoy the countryside.

Frequent leisure cyclists:

• people who will go leisure cycling approximately once or twice a fortnight during the summer, and possibly at least once or twice during the winter; they will invariably be bike owners.

Cycling enthusiasts:

• people who go leisure cycling at least once a week, whatever the time of year, although less frequently during the winter; they will be bike owners and are probably regular utility cyclists.

Family leisure cyclists:

• people for whom safety is of paramount importance; they tend to favour traffic-free cycle paths.

Occasional mountain bikers:

• people (predominantly male groups in their 20s and 30s) who go mountain biking maybe once a month; they are primarily looking for purpose-built and signed mountain bike trails.

Mountain biking enthusiasts:

• people who regularly go mountain biking; they have an older age profile than occasional mountain bikers, and still predominantly male; they will tend to plan their own routes and seek out trails using bridleways and other passable rights of way.

Source: ACK Tourism Development Services (2000), *Moving Up a Gear, a Cycle Tourism Strategy for Wales 2000–2007*, Lincoln, 7–8

Personality

The idea that a buyer and brand personality can be matched has been used as a criterion for segmentation in other sectors of marketing, especially relating to fast moving consumer goods. There has been limited application to the tourism sector. An example would be an organisation such as Club 18–30 where the choice of such a heavily branded holiday is projected specifically to reflect a fun-loving, outgoing personality. In a similar vein, segmentation using personality as a key variable is often undertaken for the degree of loyalty to the tourism product or service offering.

Multivariate segmentation

Most companies now segment the market by combining one or more of the segmentation techniques mentioned above. This involves an analysis of a combination of variables such as age, socio-economic background, geographic location and lifestyle. For example, the two linked concepts of age and life cycle have been used extensively within the tourism market. It is argued that patterns of consumption and types of holiday purchased vary considerably between the young-single segment, say those in the 18–30 age group, and the 55 plus age cohort.

Organisational segmentation

Business to business markets can also be segmented using a wide range of criteria. They describe the characteristics of the companies within the business sector, such as size or location, in a similar way to the Standard Industrial Classification (a technique used to classify companies by product group). For example, conference buyers will profile destinations according to the size of venues, accessibility, level of facilities, image and appeal.

At a micro level, companies might profile clients or other organisations according to patterns of buying, level of use or decision-making processes within the company. Thus, hotel groups will not only classify corporate clients according to the number of executives travelling on business, but also on the nature of the buying process and the overall account value. In a similar manner, destinations will segment tour operators in generating countries in accordance

with their ability to generate business volumes or to create specialist packages.

Targeting and positioning

Once the market has been segmented it is possible to target those segments that can be served effectively and profitably. This involves a reappraisal of segments according to benefits, life styles and approachability. Thus, targeting is about selecting and prioritising market segments and hence deciding the extent of market coverage. The process usually involves some form of differentiation between market segments.

Positioning refers to the way in which customers perceive a destination or company, in relation to other companies or organisations, for example, on an activity-image dimension. The key point to emphasise is that the positioning is competitive in that visitors are comparing a product, service or destination against others. At the same time, positioning has also been defined in terms of the way a company attempts to position itself in the marketplace through, for example, projection of its image, facilities, service levels and price by way of a variety of marketing communication techniques. In this context, a tourism destination or service is often multi-positioned to various market segments. Thus Britain is positioned by the British Tourist Authority as heritage, countryside activity, music and fashion according to the differing values of each market segment.

Segmentation in practice: a case study

The following case study illustrates how one tourist board has determined its approach to segmentation within its overall strategy.

The UK market remains the biggest source of tourism in Wales, and in 1998 generated 92% of all visits and 86% of all spend. This case study describes briefly the approach taken by the Wales Tourist Board (WTB) to segmenting this key market.

In order to ensure the most effective return from the application of limited marketing resources, WTB has sought to identify those segments of the UK market that offer the greatest growth potential for Wales in line with the Board's overall strategic objectives.

Target segments

The starting-off point was to classify the main UK mass market for holidays and breaks in the UK according to personal lifestyle, affluence and socio-economic status. This exercise yielded eight discrete segments. It was undertaken in the knowledge that there are significant variations between these segments in terms of the likelihood of the people in each category to take domestic holidays and the timing, frequency and value of the holidays taken.

From this evaluation, WTB identified three priority target segments and two secondary target segments, as summarised in Table 9.3.

Geographical targeting

Wales Tourist Board's main marketing campaigns are focused on priority regions, which provide the majority of visitors to Wales. These are the North West, West Midlands, M4 Corridor, South West, South, London and South East.

Niche or activity-based segments

In addition to the generic market segments listed above, WTB currently promotes a range of activity orientated tourism products to specific market segments. Following a product marketing review undertaken in 1996, individual product or activity groups were prioritised for marketing purposes as shown in Table 9.4.

Table 9.3   Priority given to target segments by the Wales Tourist Board, 2000

	Segment	Demographic profile	Priority
1	Affluent retired couples	ABC1, age 55–64 or 65+, no children in household, married/living as a couple, working part time or retired/not working, income >£15,000	Primary
2	Affluent working empty nesters	ABC1, age 45–54 or 55–64, no children in household, married/living as a couple, working part time or retired/not working, income >£25,000	Primary
3	Younger professionals	ABC1, age 25–34 or 35–44, no children in household, working full time or part time, income >£20,000	Secondary
4	Better off families, pre-school children	ABC1, age 15–24 or 25–34, with children under 5, married/living as a couple, working full time or part time, income >£20,000	Secondary
5	Better off families, school-age children	ABC1, age 25–50, married/living as couple, one or more school age children age 5–16 at home, income >£20,000	Primary
6	Lower income families	C2DE, age 25–54, dependent children all ages, unemployed or working full or part time, income <£20,000	Not a priority
7	Less well-off empty nesters	C2DE, age 45–54 or 55+, no dependent children at home, married/living as a couple or single, income <£15,000	Not a priority
8	Young rising singles or students	ACC1C2D, age 18–25, single not married, no children, student or working full or part time, income <£20,000	Not a priority

Source: personal communication with WTB

Table 9.4 Priority given to products and activity groups by the Wales Tourist Board, 1996

Product or activity	Priority
Activity holidays	Top
Walking	
Golf	
Riding	High
Cycling	
Fishing	
Gardens	
Country holidays	Medium
Arts	Low
Heritage	
Crafts	

Source: personal communication with WTB

Prioritisation determines the level of dedicated financial and human resources that the Wales Tourist Board is able to give to specific product or activity area.

Summary

Segmentation is perhaps one of the most important management concepts applied to leisure and tourism. UK government statistics on leisure and tourism form the basis for an initial analysis of the market for segmentation purposes and are widely used by practitioners in the field. The broad base of the statistical material is especially useful in evaluating overall trends and in providing an overview of the market structure. However, they have a number of limitations. They do not allow detailed segmentation in that there is a lack of customised data that can be analysed using computerised multivariate techniques such as automatic interaction detection or using a form of cluster analysis; this depends on the nature of the specific research activity. Given the greater breaking down of the traditional market segments (for example, the sun, sea and sand segment) this type of detailed analysis is required to determine more accurately the dynamics of the shifting patterns of market segmentation.

Until recently, there has been little critical appraisal of the concept of segmentation, but there are now some wide-reaching criticisms of the segmentation approach *per se*. For example, one serious misgiving is that even though segmentation techniques identify similar visitor characteristics, this does not necessarily mean that customers in a particular market segment will respond to the marketing mix in a similar manner. Another issue relates to the dynamic nature of the marketing environment. An analysis of the driving forces of tourism suggests that a continued fragmentation of markets and suppliers will make the process of segmentation more complicated in the future (Baum, 1995). One might thus conclude that it will become more difficult to segment markets according to the fundamental principles that practitioners have considered axiomatic in the past. It is argued by some that companies and destinations will increasingly adopt a marketing approach that places emphasis on personalised products and offerings targeted to small lifestyle-based segments.

Despite these criticisms, segmentation remains one of the most important marketing tools used by suppliers in the leisure and tourism sectors. Linked to targeting and positioning, it enables management teams to be able to generate achievable and in some cases profitable and appropriate (bearing in mind sustainable development) options for market and service development.

*The authors gratefully acknowledge the assistance of the Wales Tourist Board in the preparation of this chapter.

References

Aguiló, P M, Alegre, J and Riera, A (2001) 'Determinants of the price of German tourist packages on the Island of Mallorca', *Tourism Economics* 7 (1), pp. 59–74

Allin, P 'Statistics on film: what the official figures show', *Cultural Trends* 30, London, Policy Studies Institute

Baum, T (1995) 'Trends in international tourism', *Insights* 6 (Mar), pp. A117–20

Becker, G (1976) *The Economic Approach to Human Behaviour*, Chicago, The University of Chicago Press

Bowen, J T (1998) 'Market segmentation in hospitality research: no longer a sequential process', *International Journal of Contemporary Hospitality Management* 10 (7), pp. 289–96

Bramham, P (1995) 'Playing the ball, or the uses of league: class, masculinity and rugby – a case study of Sudthorpe', in G McFee et al. (eds) *Leisure Cultures: Values, Genders, Lifestyles*, Eastbourne, LSA Publications

Brown Jr, G and Henry, W (1989) *The Economic Value of Elephants*, London Environmental Economics Centre (Paper 89-12), London, University College London

Clewer, A, Pack, A D and Sinclair, M T (1992) 'Price competitiveness and inclusive tour holidays in European cities', in P Johnson and B Thomas (eds) *Choice and Demand in Tourism*, London, Mansell

Davies, B (1999) 'Industrial organisation: the UK hotel industry', *Annals of Tourism Research* 26 (2), pp. 294–311

Deaton, A and Muellbauer, J (1980a) *Economics and Consumer Behaviour*, Cambridge, Cambridge University Press

Deaton, A and Muellbauer, J (1980b) 'An almost ideal demand system', *American Economic Review* 70, pp. 312–26

De Mello, M (2001) *Theoretical and Empirical Issues in Tourism Demand Analysis*, PhD thesis, University of Nottingham

De Mello, M, Pack, A D and Sinclair, M T (2002) 'A system of equations model of UK tourism demand in neighbouring countries', *Applied Economics* 34, pp. 509–21

Downward, P M and Davies, B (2001) 'Industrial organisation and competition in the UK tour operator/travel agency business: an econometric investigation', *Journal of Travel Research* 39 (4), pp. 411–25

Downward, P M (2004) 'Assessing neoclassical microeconomic theory via leisure demand: a post Keynesian perspective', *Journal of Post Keynesian Economics*, 26 (3), pp. 37–95

Durbarry, R (2000) *Tourism Expenditure in the UK: Analysis of Competitiveness Using a Gravity-based Model* (Discussion Paper 2000/1), Nottingham, Christel DeHaan Tourism and Travel Research Institute, University of Nottingham

Durbarry, R (2002) *Long Run Tourism Demand: Error Correction Modelling and Cointegration in Demand Systems* (Discussion Paper 2002/1), Nottingham, Christel DeHaan Tourism and Travel Research Institute, University of Nottingham

Flintoff, A and Scratton, S (1995) 'Stepping into Aerobics', in G McFee et al. (eds) Leisure Cultures: Values, Genders, Lifestyles, Eastbourne, LSA Publications

Fox, K and Rickards, L (2004) Sport and Leisure: Results from the Sport and Leisure Module of the 2002 General Household Survey, London: The Stationery Office

Gershuny, J (1996) High Income People Want Less Work (ESRC Research Centre on Micro-social change Working Paper), Colchester, University of Essex

HM Treasury Forecasts for the UK Economy [annual], London, HM Treasury

Kara, A and Kaynak, E (1997) 'Markets of a single customer: exploiting conceptual developments in market segmentation', European Journal of Marketing, 31 (11), pp. 873–95

Lindberg, K and Johnson, R L (1997) 'The economic values of tourism's social impacts', Annals of Tourism Research 24 (1), pp. 90–116

Lockwood, M, Loomis, J and DeLacy, T (1993) 'A contingent valuation survey and benefit-cost analysis of forest preservation in East Gippsland, Australia', Journal of Environmental Management 38, pp. 233–43

Lumsdon, L (1997) Tourism Marketing, London, Thomson International Press

Marshall, A (1952) Principles of Economics, 8th edn, London, Macmillan

McDonald, M B H and Dunbar, I (1995) A Step By Step Approach to Creating Profitable Market Segments, London, Whitaker

Office for National Statistics Family Expenditure Survey [annual], London, The Stationery Office

Office for National Statistics (2002) Labour Market Trends, London, The Stationery Office; available at www.statistics.gov.uk/downloads/theme_labour/LMT_February02.pdf

Office for National Statistics (2003) MQ6 Transport, Travel and Tourism, Overseas Travel and Tourism, Quarter 4, 2002, London, The Stationery Office

Office for National Statistics Travel Trends – A Report on the International Passenger Survey [annual], London, The Stationery Office

Office for National Statistics (1992) UK SIC Methodological Guide, London, The Stationery Office

O'Hagan, J and Harrison, M (1984) 'Market shares of US tourist expenditure in Europe: an econometric analysis', Applied Economics 16, pp. 919–31

Papatheodorou, A (1999) 'The demand for international tourism in the Mediterranean region', Applied Economics 31, pp. 619–30

Pesaran, M H and Shin, Y (1999), Long Run Structural Modelling, DAE Working Paper No. 9419, revised version of July 1997 paper, University of Cambridge

Plog, S C (1974) 'Why destination areas rise and fall in popularity', Cornell Hotel and Restaurant Quarterly, 14 (4), pp. 55–58

Pulina, M (2002) Modelling Demand for Tourism in Italy, PhD thesis, University of Southampton

Scitovsky, T, (1976) The Joyless Economy, Oxford, Oxford University Press

Seckelmann, A (2002) 'Domestic tourism – a chance for regional development in Turkey?' Tourism Management 23, pp. 85–92

Sinclair, M T, Clewer, A and Pack A D (1990) 'Hedonic prices and the marketing of package holidays', in G Ashworth and B Goodall (eds) Marketing Tourism Places, London and New York, Routledge

Sinclair, M T and M J Stabler (1997), The Economics of Tourism, London and New York, Routledge

Smith, S L J (1995) Tourism Analysis, 2nd edn, Harlow, Longman

Song, H, Romilly, P and Liu, X (2000) 'An empirical study of outbound tourism demand in the UK', Applied Economics 32, pp. 611–24

StarUK (2002), *Statistics on Tourism and Research*; available at www.staruk.org.uk

Syriopoulos, T (1995) 'A dynamic model of demand for Mediterranean tourism', *International Review of Applied Economics* 9, pp. 318–36

Syriopoulos, T and Sinclair, M T (1993) 'An econometric study of tourism demand: the AIDS model of US and European tourism in Mediterranean countries', *Applied Economics* 25, pp. 1541–52

Thomas, M et al. (1998) *Living in Britain: Results from the 1996 General Household Survey*, London, The Stationery Office

Turner, L W and Reisinger Y (2001) 'Shopping satisfaction for domestic tourists', *Journal of Retailing and Consumer Services* 8, pp. 15–27

Veblen, T (1925) *The Theory of the Leisure Class*, London, Allen and Unwin

Wales Tourist Board (2000) *Achieving our Potential – A Tourism Strategy for Wales*, Cardiff, Wales Tourist Board

White, K J (1982) *The Demand for International Travel: a System-wide Analysis for US Travel to Western Europe* (Discussion Paper No. 82-28), Vancouver, University of British Columbia

World Tourism Organisation *Compendium of Tourism Statistics* [annual], World Tourism Organisation, Madrid

Index

Note: page numbers in **bold** indicate figures or tables.